Heart-Stirring Medicine of Korean Temple Food

Wisdom & Recipes by a Zen Buddhist Monk

Venerable Dae-Ahn

ALPHA SISTERS PUBLISHING

Alpha Sisters Publishing, LLC
5174 McGinnis Ferry Road #348
Alpharetta, GA 30005
alphasisterspublishing.com

This book is published with the support of Publication Industry Promotion Agency of Korea (KPIPA).

Original Korean Edition, 대안스님의 마음설레는 레시피, published in 2012 by Gimm-Young Publishers, Inc.

English Edition, *Heart-Stirring Medicine of Korean Temple Food: Wisdom & Recipes by a Zen Buddhist Monk*, published in 2024 by Alpha Sisters Publishing, arranged by Gimm-Young Publishers, Inc.

Written by Venerable Dae-Ahn
Translator: Loni Kim
Editors: E. Ce Miller, Emily Han
Publisher: Seo Choi
Book Designer: Ruth Kokila
Foreword & Recipe Translation: Hyosun Ro

Library of Congress Cataloging-in-Publication Data is available upon request.

First Edition
ISBN 979-8-9869373-4-2 (Paperback)
ISBN 979-8-9869373-5-9 (e-book)

Printed in the United States of America

Contents

Foreword

I was introduced to the wonders of Korean temple food in 2015 when the Buddhist Television Network of Korea (BTN) invited me to appear in a documentary about Korean temple cuisine and its globalization. The network was interested in my perspective as a Korean cooking blogger in the US. While filming, I tried my hand at cooking a few temple dishes using recipes provided by the film crew. The dishes made a lasting impression on me. How could something seemingly so simple taste so refined?

Eager to learn more, I began reading temple cookbooks, including those by the Venerable Dae-Ahn. During my visits to Korea, I even took a cooking class from a well-known temple chef and enjoyed dining at restaurants specializing in temple food. One of those restaurants was Balwoo Gongyang, Michelin-starred and then headed by the Venerable Dae-Ahn. Dining at Balwoo Gongyang was an unforgettable culinary experience. Over the years, inspired by my forays into temple cuisine, I wrote several blog posts introducing Korean temple food to my audience.

What makes Korean temple food different from other Korean dishes? In short, temple cuisine primarily consists of seasonal vegetables and fruits grown on temple grounds or harvested from surrounding fields and mountains. Other vegetables common to traditional Korean cooking are prohibited in temple cuisine, including garlic, scallions, and chives, which are considered stimulants that hinder spiritual meditation. Temple kitchens only use natural seasonings. In an era of commercial mass production, temples maintain the traditional practice of making their own seasonings, such as *doenjang* (fermented soybean paste) and *ganjang* (soy sauce). Temple food is seasoned lightly, inviting the diner to focus on the ingredients' natural flavors and textures. Most importantly, what sets temple cuisine apart is its emphasis on cultivating a harmonious connection between oneself, nature, and others.

Heart-Stirring Medicine of Korean Temple Food is much more than a cookbook. The Venerable Dae-Ahn eloquently writes about the history, philosophy, and principles of Korean temple cuisine, informed by her lifelong journey of learning about and teaching the art of temple food. She delves into the characteristics and healing properties of many temple ingredients with related stories and tips on using them. Her passion for sharing her knowledge and love of temple cuisine with a wider audience is truly admirable.

I had the privilege of helping translate the recipes in this book. As I worked on each recipe, I included helpful information for readers new to Korean cooking and potential substitutions for ingredients that may be harder to find outside Korea. There's a clear shortage of English-language books on Korean temple food, and I am very grateful to the Venerable Dae-Ahn and the publishing team for this much-needed book. You will learn so much from it. Whether you are Buddhist, vegan, health conscious, or simply interested in Korean culture, this is must-read. Just as it did for me, this book will inspire you to reassess your approach to cooking, eating, and connecting with others through food.

Hyosun Ro
Author of the blog *Korean Bapsang, a Korean Mom's Home Cooking*
May 2024

Translator's Reflection

I first met the Venerable Dae-Ahn in March of 2023 when I went to visit her temple at Jirisan. The plum blossoms were in bloom, signaling spring. We took a walk around the mountains where she showed me the flowers, the brown soil, and plants sprouting on the side of the road. I watched as she plucked a plum blossom to invite to tea with us, and knew from that moment on that everything in the book is exactly as it is experienced. The words are without additives, as are the dishes.

Our world today is full of sensory distractions of all kinds. To let nature take her course and allow the scents and flavors to speak for themselves was not such a revolutionary idea in the past, yet today people the world over visit our monks to seek the wisdom of this tradition. My hope for the English edition of this book is that it will help us all to remember what it truly means to return to the earth, to care for ourselves and our neighbors, and to give each other the nourishment we all need.

The preface to this book is also its heart. For this reason, it is full of native Korean names of plants to retain the poetry and beauty of its original passages. It is as if the words rise straight from the soil to be delivered directly to our hearts. Hopefully, it will make you feel as if you're standing right atop the beauty and majesty of our ancestral lands.

Loni Kim
December 2023

A
Welcoming
Table

Communicating Happiness Through Food

When you live in a temple, teatime is your most leisurely hour. Just as Uisun[1] prescribed, I gently placed a bridalwreath spirea branch atop the sacred meditation space, having carefully picked it to set as the tea flower. Tradition says that placing a flower at the tea table perpetuates the sentiments of our good ancestors who would invite a single flower to tea to deepen their appreciation for the sanctity of life and complement the scent of the tea. The flower's presence invokes clarity in our hearts and helps us find more ease, propriety, and contentment as we sip our tea.

Twenty years ago, I came to the Guemsuam Temple in Mount Jirisan, determined to continue my practice as a monk quietly and privately away from the world. While at the temple, I've simultaneously felt the suffering of both being in and apart from the world. Now, I'm making food in a monk's habit. I've become a busy monk, traveling back and forth between Korea and the rest of the world while experimenting with temple cuisine, giving lectures, and even appearing on TV. Cooking has been my joy from the moment I first served bean curd *kimchi* soup to a *bosal-nim*, a female devotee, who braved the frigid wind to visit my mountain cave and offer me rice. Serving food to visitors of Guemsuam Temple has become my greatest happiness.

---

1 Known in Korea as Cho-ui Seonsa (초의선사), Uisun was a 19th-century Zen Buddhist monk who introduced the philosophy and practice of tea.

But how did I end up becoming a culinary monk? For a long time, I sought to understand why I chose to cook from all the various paths of service. I also wanted to know why the infinitely compassionate Buddha did not allow the consumption of all types of food and what made him deem certain foods unsuitable for humans. Slowly but surely, I started to gain more insight. The laws of fate dictate that one is born in a particular location, lives on that land, and follows its customs and traditions—including one's diet.

Understood this way, temple food is the manifestation of food culture from the heavens.

Preparing temple cuisine is a practice of creating meals that are less harmful to life, offer gratitude to life, and give one more integrity in following the path of the Buddha. It is the connection between the chef and her ingredients and between the food and the people who eat it. By preparing and consuming temple cuisine, you become more peaceful, knowing that because you're causing less harm to others in this life, you won't be harmed in the next one. Although the food is incredibly humble and unremarkably natural, every morsel is instilled with the philosophy of utmost respect for all life.

How could I not be grateful that this is the role I've been given?

First, I purified my heart. Next, I embraced an attitude of loving all life. Then, I began the work of raising public awareness that we must all share this mindset when making our food. We must also consider the harmony between natural ingredients, ensuring those with strong traits blend well with milder ones. All foods must be made delicately, with one's whole heart.

I've spent many busy days sharing the art of traditional temple cuisine while developing it further to make it more palatable to the world. It took ten years of study in food nutrition to receive a doctorate as a mature university student. I studied the science behind food and the consilience of various food studies in order to teach temple cuisine properly. The life of a monk, specifically that of a monk who cooks, hasn't always been easy. But just as a bud penetrates the frozen earth and overcomes harsh winds to grow and blossom into fresh fruit, and just as every long-awaited meal undergoes a period of preparation to become life-giving sustenance, I, too was able to overcome hard times by carrying the hope that I could share the taste of connection through food.

People who experience temple food for the first time are often thrown off by the simple scents and flavors of these unfamiliar ingredients. But they soon smile lightly as they eat *gondalbi ssambap* and *dureup jeonbyeong*, expressing surprise at the taste of a veggie "ham" sandwich and fried mushrooms. Watching children fill with delight while munching on a rice burger, rice cake, and potato pizza or witnessing foreigners give a thumbs-up while awkwardly holding *kimchi yangjangpi* and vegetarian *jajangmyeon* noodles between chopsticks made me see that temple food has already become as accepted as one-breath with many in the world. Whenever I hear someone say that their heart and mind are at peace and that they gained more understanding by slowly reducing their meat consumption and switching to a plant-based diet, I become joyful that a table laden with food can be a messenger of peace. I cook every day to share joy, love, and ease.

I find there's no time to rest as I continue to share temple food with more and more people, including the plain meals served during a monk's training and the bountiful dishes showcasing the diversity of nature. I travel to the mountains, fields, and islands to search for ingredients that align with the mind, body, and spirit. Then, I season, fry, boil, steam, and parch as I develop and prepare dishes, experimenting with food. I live in joyful table meditation as I diligently prepare, share, and communicate through food. This food I make without rest is the food of "emptiness." I'm not cooking food so much as I'm practicing emptying my mind.

My days are busy as I meet people through food and become one with the world, protecting the respect and love of life. When I first received an invitation to appear on a well-known Korean documentary show, I politely declined because, as a monk, I questioned the wisdom of sharing myself to that extent with the people of the world. However, over time, I realized that introducing temple food to a global audience creates a thread of connection through the sanctity of countless lives. This is my role and responsibility.

I started writing this book hoping that, metaphorically, the spirit of ease and contentment that comes from placing a flower at a tea table would blossom into happiness. Though I've given many lectures, studied rigorously, made media appearances, and am now in charge of operations at Balwoo Gongyang—a restaurant in Seoul specializing in temple cuisine—I now experience no disturbance in my mind. I suppose my mind has become as light as the natural flavors of temple food.

Despite my humble writing skills, I've written this book to raise awareness about the right attitude we must carry when cooking, how we must greet and eat food, and how this culinary practice can benefit anyone's life. It contains my humble beliefs and vision for the future of temple cuisine. Just as temple food is made simply from common ingredients directly from the environment, my plain and simple words carry nothing special. Yet I write with a heart full of gratitude for those who have always stood beside me like the abundance of nature herself so that I may carry on this practice and for all who have eaten my food with joy, as well as the critics who have given me a spicier taste, so that I could concentrate further in my studies.

Now, let me set a table of food with a pure, fluid, and plentiful heart.

The Buddha's Table

What wind will breeze past me today? Which bird will peck at the food offering on the ceremonial stone in the front yard? Who will visit this valley to fill their empty hearts and bodies?

On a clear spring day like today, with the sky showing its face, I want to roll up my sleeves and roam around the hills full of the scent of spring to forage for wild greens. Perhaps we anticipate the arrival of spring for its life-giving nature. I'm no exception, as I cook cleansing food anew daily to share its fresh energy.

When I'm sitting and drinking tea with a plum blossom friend the wind has carried my way, leaves and wild green mountain herbs reach out their light green hands, calling out to me with their gestures. Mount Jirisan raises me up like this each spring, her earth bountiful with sun-laden sprouts. In April, the mountain holds an incredibly bright and radiant spring feast. Amidst the windy chaos of cherry blossom petals, pink rhododendrons smile like newlyweds, and sticky-sweet honey pours from the yellow petals of Chinese peashrub. The potent scents of spicebush and peonies from the valley make me forget my weariness as I climb the mountain. When I raise my head briefly to look out onto the valley, pink peach blossoms make my heart flutter, and the sight of wild cherry tree petals spread out in white among the light green forest is an absolute wonder to behold.

It's hard to move along for the joy of watching these mountain herbs poking their heads out from the trees and ground as if to compete with the feast of flowers. Stonecrop seeds carried by the breeze form a green carpet atop the hill, while butterburs create a field beside it. Butterbur is a plant that can penetrate a still-wintry earth and contains enough heat to melt the remaining snow surrounding it. To gather this plant, you cut from the bottom of the stem. Its rosy, magenta base is bittersweet and crunchy, ideal for lightly blanching, seasoning, or pickling. Shepherd's purse can be found between the butterburs, its roots so sturdy their scent comes from deep within the earth. There's nothing like putting them in a *doenjang jjigae* or brewing the best-smelling shepherd's purse tea to savor the taste of spring.

Because Mount Jirisan also suffers from pollution caused by frequent footsteps and human hands, one must go further into the mountain to find sprouts from a wild angelica tree or castor aralia. The castor aralia is a cousin of the angelica tree and is commonly called *eongaenamu* in Gyeongsangdo. *Eongaenamu* is difficult to gather due to its thorns, but the scent is so thick it's intoxicating just to get near it. Like angelica, *eongaenamu* can be blanched slightly and dipped in *gochujang*. Its bitter taste is so unique that the people of Hadong often say, "You can buy the sprout of an *eongaenamu* with the money you get for selling an angelica tree," or "If you find an *eongaenamu* sprout, you've got yourself a meal." On a lucky day, I might even see some *deulmi* sprouts, which people say you will only taste once or twice in your entire life. *Deulmi's* shape resembles a combination of angelica and the tree of heaven, and it's tender, sweet, and tasty. But because it's a protected plant, it costs a heavy price if simply gathered at will.

Walking around the mountain like this, I feel like I'm on a treasure hunt, taking one step to greet spring mugwort, another to meet *sanchi* and *gomchi,* and the tastily bitter *gondalbi* beside it. Each step reveals a new treasure. Adding henbit, with its stunning colors, daylilies, leaves from the tree of heaven, and dandelion on top, my basket fills up with spring in just a few hours.

I make haste for Seoul as I carry the spring of the mountain with me. It's a relief to share this spring scent at Balwoo Gongyang—I imagine the expressions on people's faces when they greet the springtime through my cuisine. *Thump.* My heart beats at the thought. It's been thirty years since I've shaved my head, and still, my heart beats.

The Recipe of My Life

My old life flashes before my eyes like moving images on a kaleidoscope as I head to Seoul.

"Why did you become a monk?"
"How old were you when you became a monk?"
"How did you get into temple cuisine?"

These are the most common questions I have received since becoming a monk. The life I had before shaving my head and becoming a disciple of the Buddha may as well be a past life. Still, people seem to be very curious about it. I could make up a sad, dramatic story that young high school girls may enjoy, but what's past is already gone! It's true that I once had the life of a student, a social life, and a period of training with a fellow practitioner. But time also kept flowing, and now I am where I am.

If I think about my past, my first memory is that of my mother. She passed away when I was just nine years old, leaving behind ten of us siblings. At her burial, on New Year's Eve, the bus transporting us got stuck in the snow, and we clutched onto our mother's coffin, crying for her short fifty years on earth. I have a vivid memory of carrying the funeral bier with my frozen body and burying my mother in a wintry field of snow. My face was frozen blue in the furious wind, and I buried it in my father's black coat, shivering as I cried my heart out. My cousins and friends took pity on me as they watched me stand by my mother, wearing mourning clothes at such a young age. A heartfelt epitaph was placed before my mother's grave. For the next three years, I rushed to my mother, pedaling to her gravesite on my sister's bike. After that, I clung tightly to the emptiness where her presence had been for a long time. Even as I write this now, my eyes fill with tears as I think of her, and my heart cries for the brief time I had with my beautiful and benevolent mother. Now, I'm over fifty years old, but I still miss her, this woman who once had so many mouths to feed yet still found time to look after the poor— whenever the beggars in front of Jeonju Station begged for food, she never looked down on them. Instead, she treated them like guests, serving food on a small round dining table called *doraesang*. Looking back, it's clear that my mother was someone who knew the beauty of sharing, the sanctity of life, and the connection food could bring.

Growing up without my mother meant my life was always cold. My stepmother soon joined the household, and our financial struggles grew worse. As I entered puberty, I didn't want to return home after school, and my head was full of doubtful, depressing thoughts about how I would live. I suffered a lot during that time—is youth always so full of suffering? Even after graduating high school and becoming a member of society, finding meaning in my life wasn't easy, and I wasn't happy at work. I felt like a part of my heart was empty, like I wasn't on the right path and was merely floundering in life's fog.

If I hadn't met my teacher, who watched over me with interest, my aimless wandering would have been prolonged. At that time, she was training to become a nun, and I started attending the Catholic church through her influence. For a time, I decided to become a nun as well. When that didn't happen, I then set my mind on living alone because my *saju*[2] predicted

---

2 *Saju* (사주), meaning "four pillars," is the Korean practice of studying one's fate and fortune according to the cycle of yin and yang and the five elements.

I wouldn't be able to maintain a long marriage. I didn't want to leave any child I might have to such a sad fate as I'd experienced in losing my mother—that would have been unbearable. I had grown up accustomed to seeing the adults in my life leave, one by one. As a result, I understood death earlier and more deeply than others. *Why couldn't we live as long as we wanted?* I wondered. I had learned about the futility of life too soon and was already on my own.

But as my feelings of futility slowly started to fade, I finally began to see the shape of my life. I turned towards the temple and settled on taking the path of a monk. Since I had spent a lot of time reflecting on death due to the deaths of those around me, I decided to devote myself to the practice as if I hadn't been born at all. I went to Haeinsa, a temple my older sister had attended to become a monk four years earlier.

Every year, family members visited me with looks of concern. Each time, I told them I'd return home when I wanted and sent them back with reminders not to worry about me. Time unfolded faster than I thought, and for ten years, I renewed my fate of being a monk over and over amidst strife and feelings of selfishness. I set aside my desire to spontaneously run away and waited for the karmic storm to pass. Finally, my family resigned themselves to my fate and encouraged me to become a good monk. Twenty-seven years have passed without a pause in my practice, though the process was full of fierce intensity. Today, I'm living the life of a specialized monk under the banner of temple cuisine.

"Seunim, my mouth is full of spring."

The morning after I arrived in Seoul carrying a bucketful of spring in my arms, I was greeted by the sight of some pitifully blackened mugwort.
I had made sure to check all the ingredients before storing them in the fridge, yet their freshness had vanished without a trace. It was my fault for telling the chefs we should make mugwort soup in the morning. Because of this, our youngest chef had washed and prepared the mugwort the night before.

All plants start dying as soon as they are touched by human hands. Putting a knife to a plant means to kill it. Root plants like *deodeok*[3] and lotus root take a long time to prep and aren't as affected if you prepare them in advance, but green plants rapidly lose their vivacity the minute they're washed and cut. The same goes for mugwort, even though it's a tenacious plant—you must wrap it in paper and avoid washing it until the last minute. But an inexperienced chef had only thought of their own convenience and prepared it beforehand.

I raised my voice against the chefs. It may seem like a small mistake to wash mugwort in advance, but it's a critical detail regarding a chef's attitude, which gets transferred directly to the person eating the food. The primary ingredient of any chef is care, which enables us to look after every small detail. When it comes to cooking, technique is not wisdom. Instead,

---

3 *Deodeok* (더덕): codonopsis root. *Deodeok* and *doraji* (도라지, bellflower root) are both used in Korean traditional cuisines and known to have medicinal and health benefits.

a chef's wisdom comes from knowing how to cook the freshest, most tasty, and most nutritious food, true to the nature of the ingredients.

People may not notice that the mugwort isn't as fresh as it could be. But food isn't about the taste at the end of your tongue. To mistreat an ingredient by taking an easier shortcut is to disrespect both the mugwort and the person eating the food. Some people may say I'm making too big a deal out of mugwort, but we must remember the precious nature within every blade of grass and mugwort leaf and honor their toil with gratitude.

Since the old days, mugwort soup has been a seasonal food used to greet the coming of spring. The green of the plant contains a bitter taste that awakens one from the stagnant energy of winter. Those of the wealthier class would add egg and meat to the mugwort soup, while in the temple, soybean paste was added to help overcome spring fever and gain energy to combat the approaching summer heat. Eating mugwort means receiving a potent medicine strong enough to penetrate the cold, frozen earth. In terms of nutrition, mugwort contains vitamins A and C, magnesium, calcium, and potassium, which are effective for preventing minor ailments like colds. Since mugwort warms a cold stomach, it helps ease constipation, supports reproductive health, and is an anti-inflammatory agent that reduces fever and heat. It's not a minor mistake to serve mugwort that has lost its vivacity, just for the sake of convenience.

All life is precious, and nothing in this world isn't filled with Buddhahood. That's why the Buddha spoke of the innate sanctity that exists in all creation. It lives in the air that can neither be seen nor grasped. It lives in a single chirping bird. It lives in a nameless blade of grass.

Simply put, everything that contains life or attempts to create life holds the nature of the Buddha. Everything that appears in the world or enables something to appear is born with its own special mission. It's important to protect the inherent nature of every particle of creation because all these things carry the essence of the Buddha—essentially, this is to say that we are all Buddhas. It's just that there are awakened Buddhas and Buddhas who have not yet awakened. Buddhas who have not yet awakened can learn about the nature of fate and enter nirvana to attain Buddhahood. This is called Practice.

So, how do you walk the path of Practice?

The path of Practice is a life without male and female genders; last names like Kim, Lee, and Park; distinguished people and unremarkable people; people you like and people you don't; ideas of precious people and worthless people; "my family" and "your family;" discrimination between people, plants, and animals; and discrimination between you and me. It is the fading away of distinction resulting in the objective and subjective perspective. The Buddha's teaching of the Middle Way eliminates concepts like "me" and "mine," which signifies equality. The moment we believe that all creation carries the nature of Buddha and that nothing can exist without equality or sanctity, we experience a change of heart. Our hearts become as generous as the Buddha, who considers all creation precious and beautiful. The name "Buddha" can be thought of as synonymous with benevolence, love, and profound wisdom, and we need only receive the meaning it carries with our hearts to attain its vast universality. As the sun

in the sky always watches over us, it opens a world of immeasurable light in which our hearts always watch over us as well.

If you sense you might understand this, but don't know how to put it into practice, try the following: First, nod your head. If you feel that there's nothing that isn't precious in this world, nod your head. Nod again if you see that the air in the atmosphere, a single bird, a small insect, and a nameless blade of grass all carry life. Nod as you slowly think about the sanctity of such life. Nod if you feel gratitude for all the things that give us life. When we treat all sacred creation with gratitude, in service of the Buddha, we naturally walk the path of Practice, of nirvana.

Furthermore, when we realize that all those things make the next life possible, we are naturally filled with gratitude. This is becoming the Buddha. So, when we see that the mugwort was born somewhere in the foothills of Mount Jirisan to give us health, the mugwort becomes the Buddha: an entity we must serve. When we think that each ingredient we encounter carries the nature of Buddha, we can't treat anything carelessly. If we cook food intending to help each ingredient reveal its inherent nature—its Buddhahood—we can extract its nutrition as well as its taste.

When I enter the kitchen in the afternoon, after the busy breakfast and lunch hours of Balwoo Gongyang, I can clearly see the chefs' nervousness. Although the hustle of morning has already passed like the Buddha's smile, they still seem to be carrying it in their hearts. The sight makes me feel slightly sorry. It's also endearing. I only use firm words as one method of teaching. I walk to the fridge to implement yet another. There, I find some untouched wild leaves, still wrapped exactly as I had left them, probably because they are an unfamiliar ingredient. I take out the bundle to wash it, then sift some flour, wishing for the kitchen to fill with laughter as green as the leaves. The freshly sprouted winged spindle leaves are soft yet chewy. To preserve their nature, I combine only a small amount of batter and perilla oil, coating the leaves and pan-frying them lightly. The chefs stand beside me, busily taking notes with reddened cheeks, while the young one who prepared the mugwort nervously listens to my instructions. Finally, I take a corner from the first fried leaf, dip it in a bit of sauce, and push it into their mouth. They smiles brightly with reddened ears.

"*Seunim*, my mouth is full of spring."

Mugwort & Root Rice Cake

(Ssuk Beomuri Bburi Tteok)

It's best to use young mugwort harvested in spring. Mugwort harvested in the fall is sometimes eaten, but fall mugwort is better suited for therapeutic applications such as moxibustion or baths. Boil and freeze spring mugwort. It will keep well for up to a year. On white rice flour, green mugwort, red beet, and yellow sweet potato reflect the colors of the five elements. The rice cake is not just colorful, but it's also tastier and healthier than plain or mugwort-only rice cakes.

Ingredients

4 ounces *ssuk* (Korean mugwort, *Artemisia princeps*)

1.5 ounces *goguma* (Korean sweet potato)

1.5 ounces beet

5 chestnuts, peeled

5.5 ounces *ssalgaru* (wet rice flour[1])

1 tablespoon sugar

½ teaspoon salt

2 tablespoons water

---

1 In Korea, rice flour for this type of rice cake is made by soaking short-grain rice overnight, draining, and taking to a gristmill to get it ground. The resulting rice flour has a higher level of moisture content than dry rice flour. In the US, you may find ready-made wet rice flour for rice cakes in the freezer section of Korean grocery stores

Directions

1. When foraging mugwort, be aware of look-alike plants. If the roots are purplish, they are not mugwort. Wash the mugwort in cold water several times and drain. If the sprigs are too long, cut them into shorter pieces.

2. Dice the sweet potato and beet into approximately ½-inch pieces. Soak the beet in cold water for 30 minutes and pat dry with a paper towel to remove excess moisture. This process helps prevent the color from transferring to the other ingredients. Dice the peeled chestnuts into similar-sized pieces.

3. Sift the rice flour. Add the sugar, salt, and water and mix everything together well.

4. Add the mugwort, sweet potato, beet, and chestnut and toss gently to combine.

5. Set up a steamer with water in the bottom. Line the steamer insert with a cheesecloth and bring the steamer to a boil. When steam rises, place the mixture in the steamer insert, spreading it evenly. Cover and steam for 10 to 15 minutes on high heat. Do not overcook the mugwort.

6. Remove the rice cake from the steamer and peel off the cheesecloth to serve.

Mountain Vegetables Sushi

(Sanyacho Chobap)

While we tend to associate sushi with fish, there are limitless toppings you can add to seasoned rice balls that are not fish or other seafood. Experiment with various seasonal vegetables, in different colors, that you enjoy.

Ingredients

9 ounces uncooked brown rice

2 ounces *sseumbagwi* (toothed ixeridium) roots or parsnip

5 to 6 *dureup* (angelica tree) shoots or asparagus tips

2 *deodeok* (codonopsis) roots or *ueong* (burdock) roots

Salt, sugar, white vinegar, *gukganjang* (soup soy sauce[1]), sesame oil for seasoning

Wasabi (Asian horseradish) and soy sauce for serving

Sweet vinegar for sushi rice:

¼ cup white vinegar

2 tablespoons sugar

½ tablespoon salt

---

1 Also known as *jibganjang* (homemade soy sauce) and *Joseon ganjang*, *gukganjang* (soup soy sauce) is a soy sauce that's traditionally made at home with fermented soybean blocks and salt brine as a by-product of making *doenjang* (fermented soybean paste). It's lighter in color than regular soy sauce but has a rich, savory taste. *Gukganjang* is commercially available at Korean markets

Seasoning sauce for *deodeok:*

1 tablespoon *gochujang*

1 tablespoon *jocheong* (rice syrup)

1 teaspoon sesame oil

Directions

1. Prepare the sweet vinegar for sushi rice. Mix the vinegar, sugar, and salt in a small saucepan and simmer over low heat until the sugar is dissolved. Set aside.

2. Cook the rice. The cooked rice should be fluffy. While the rice is cooking, prepare the mountain vegetables.

3. Wash and drain the *sseumbagwi* roots and marinate them in 1 teaspoon each of salt, sugar, and vinegar while preparing the other vegetables. This process removes the bitterness of *sseumbagwi* while seasoning it.

4. Blanch the *dureup* quickly in salted boiling water, rinse in cold water, and drain. Season lightly with the soup soy sauce and sesame oil.

5. For the *deodeok*, remove the skin, then gently flatten the root with a rolling pin by pounding it down gently. Make the seasoning sauce by mixing together the *gochujang*, rice syrup, and sesame oil. Brush the *deodeok* with the seasoning sauce, and then pan-fry.

6. While the rice is hot, add the sweet vinegar mixture and fold gently until the mixture coats the rice evenly. Once the rice cools down, put a spoonful of rice on your palm and squeeze to form an oval-shaped ball. Top with a bit of wasabi and one of the prepared vegetable ingredients for each rice ball. There will be three different colors and textures.

7. Serve with some wasabi and soy sauce for dipping. Once in your mouth, you will be joyfully awakened to the taste and fragrance of spring.

part one
A Healing Table

Every season, nature provides us with what we need in abundance and diversity. From the midnight sun of the Arctic to the Antarctic land of penguins, nature never ceases to give. She suffers illnesses brought on by humans and heals herself repeatedly as she coexists with us. We live together in this universe like comrades on the same spiritual path. So, we must become mutually beneficial partners. We could both be in danger if we don't help one another—becoming extinct if we only put ourselves first without compassion, insight, and wisdom. But if we understand each other well, we will live in peaceful harmony.

The most evident example of this presents itself softly but strikes with a significant impact: disease. Whether mental or physical, illness causes suffering and incites us to strive to relieve that suffering. But what makes us fall into this trap of disease? And how can we escape its seemingly never-ending cycle and live in health and happiness at last?

The Food in Our Hearts

Guemsuam Temple receives many visitors who are cancer patients, coming here with the hope that they will be able to cure their illness by visiting us. Since I'm a naturalist, not a doctor, I believe we can cure diseases with food. But it's not possible to receive everyone who wishes to come. There's not enough space, and teaching the right mindset and regimen required to cure each unique body and disease is difficult. It's impossible to change the course of an illness that has taken many days to form in a single visit. It's also very challenging to help patients who are not only diseased in body but also in their minds, to guide them toward looking after each of their sensitive and self-centered spirits. We can find ourselves on opposite ends of the spectrums of health and illness, happiness and suffering, depending on what we put in the bowls of our hearts. So, the question is, with what will we fill that bowl?

Disease is born of five basic desires that have pooled in the bowl for too long—those of food, sleep, sex, money, and fame. These constitute the Five Desires. Of these, the desire for food is experienced by most people: we humans can't help but continuously search for food to survive. Since this is fundamental animal nature, it's one of our most difficult desires to escape. But the lust for food that goes beyond our basic survival can upset the balance in our body and lead us to disease. Simply regulating one's appetite can help to manage the other four desires, so the ability to rein in one's desire for food generates tremendous power. This means it's imperative to balance our meals. Deciding how and what to eat is the key to achieving this balance.

Each person's physical limitations will differ, but if you can control your appetite, you can also manage your desire for sleep. Although sleep is necessary to rest and recharge our bodies for further activity, it can also be a product of our desire for laziness. Excessive sleep can pollute our minds. It possesses the power to make us slothful, drench us in delusion, and make us feel depressed. Therefore, according to the wisdom principles of yin and yang and the Five Element Theory, we must go to bed and allow our mind and body to rest when the sun sets.[1] It's just as important to get the right amount of sleep as it is to eat neither too much nor too little.

Sex is also a human desire born of the need to reproduce. But the hunger I'm addressing here doesn't refer to the propellant desire to preserve the species but rather the seeking of sensory pleasure. This search can scratch away at one's soul and lead to exhaustion. On occasion, the private sex life of a famous person will be shared with the public through a smartphone or the internet. This kind of social phenomenon is an extreme example of immature sexual desire. Spying on another's private life for entertainment is a terrible sign that society has fallen into voyeurism like that portrayed in the film *The Truman Show*. Without a true philosophy of respect for life and a love of humanity, we can all become slaves to our senses, trapped in the endless desire for sensory fulfillment.

The desire for wealth and fame is formed on a foundation that depends on stepping over others. It is a conscious, evolutionary societal desire rather than an inherent human desire. This type of desire comes from a lack of insight that mistakenly identifies that which isn't us with ourselves.

---

1 See Part Two of this book for detailed information on yin and yang and the Five Element Theory

It is a highly potent desire that causes stress and depression for modern humans and leads to heartsickness and mental illness. When one's heart and mind are tired, one's body is also exhausted, ultimately leading to suffering from disease.

If we approach this psychologically, any desire that leads to suffering is caused by an insecure mind. Buddha said that a single life was born 8,000 times in this world. This is no different from saying that there are 8,000 diverse selves within each of us. This may sound like we all have multiple personalities, but living in this contemporary world, we often encounter various situations where we behave differently. For instance, our voices change when we answer the phone. It's easy to witness such a swift shift in personality in the context of a phone call. We all have different selves depending on the person or situation we encounter, and these selves also change according to perceived benefit. Sometimes, there are so many selves we don't know that it creates confusion. When this happens, we may exclaim, *Why am I like this?* or *Why am I living like this?* and resign ourselves to the inevitability of this phenomenon. In the case of Korea, it is a society that includes many contexts requiring a different self—so much so that perhaps one person finds use for all 8,000 selves in a single moment! The self that contains negative traits like selfishness, contentiousness, bias, arrogance, degradation, blasphemy, violation of human rights, untrustworthiness, and self-righteousness is commingling with the self that is filled with the opposite traits: freedom, equality, peace, respect, love, friendship, satisfaction, generosity, and tranquility.

But as it is said, one must know one's enemy to win the battle. So, if we can inspect the cause of our suffering, we can also find the cure. When we are willing to look into ourselves, our hearts and minds become strong, wise, and able to withstand any poison. So, what is poison, and what is medicine when it comes to one's heart and mind?

Tam (탐): The Poison of Gluttony

It might seem curious that a monk who cooks temple food first addresses the heart and mind. But all food grows from the garden of our hearts and serves as fertilizer, so this topic is like a meal that can't be skipped. There are three types of poison that must not taint the mind: *tam* (탐, greed/attachment), *jin* (진, anger/aversion), and *chi* (치, delusion/ignorance). The most universal is *tam*, or covetous desire. When we desire something, it creates a false, tainted sense of self. The need to protect this false self incites more greed, which mistakes ambition for happiness. When this desire is unfulfilled, we suffer in anguish and torment. It wouldn't be an exaggeration to say that this kind of mindset starts with gluttony, though we often don't give this much thought.

I, myself, was gripped by gluttony once—and it still makes me smile to think of my time at the Bongnyeong Temple in Gangwon Province. In those days, I was always hungry, no matter how much I ate. At mealtimes, we were only given ten minutes to eat, and I could never empty my rice bowl after filling it to the brim. We also had to fetch hot water from the middle of the hall, which added to my running out of time. I stuffed so much rice into my bowl that I'd still be eating while the other monks were washing their bowls or when the head monk announced the end of mealtime with the thwack of a bamboo stick. I was like a little chick crying that there wasn't enough food. But I wasn't alone. Many of us younger monks found ourselves still busily eating at the end of mealtime, partly because there wasn't a lot of food to go around, causing us to load our bowls full. Also, our studies often included reading aloud the whole day, making us both nervous and hungry. Still, I didn't always eat according to my hunger level; instead, I'd consume a pile of rice without hesitation, thinking I'd be hungry.

At teatime, teachers and pupils would gather around to drink tea and chat over light refreshments. I hid the refreshments in my clothes to save for later. But as the day went on, I'd forget that I hid them or where I put them, allowing them to spoil because I left them out too long. Why was it so hard to let go of my craving for food?

Looking back, I can see that it was foolishness that brought on my appetite, but I also believe that I can thank my past actions for helping me live a life of emptiness today. Because I've filled my belly to the brim, I now know there's no reason to do so. That's not to say that one only needs to open one's eyes to the foolishness of greed by fulfilling one's desire first. Instead, it shows that within all of us is the nature of the Buddha, which bestows us with the wisdom to learn from our follies. To do so, we must observe our desires in more detail. Which desires threaten to catch us in their grip?

In the past, we had to grit our teeth and live ferociously to create the energy required to survive under extremely harsh conditions. In Korea, it's only been since the 1990s that we've been able to experience our current food culture of abundance and excess. Korea is a unique example of a country that has changed its relationship with food over a very short period of time. Even places like the countries of the Middle East, Japan, India, or Europe haven't gone through such rapid transformation. In the old days, Koreans had to wait for special feasts to enjoy fatty foods or seasonal specialties that filled our bodies with necessary protein. It was unimaginable that every street corner would feature restaurants serving meat and alcohol like there are today—and even more unthinkable is the explosion of dining-out and delivery culture.

Perhaps we've fallen into an even greater hedonism than what the Roman emperor Nero enjoyed. We buy shoes of all shapes for every season and dress to suit our style, adorning our heads with golden accessories. We wish to change our faces to resemble celebrities and take countless health supplements to increase energy. We say these things are necessary to help maintain our dignity, but they are merely symptoms of our desire to shape outward appearances. Even at the meal table, we display greedy behavior left and right. Leftover food is thrown in the trash; there are no qualms about discarding soup. It's even less common to find people who feel responsible for the fact that food waste pollutes the environment. Nowhere is this greedy attitude more apparent than in the refrigerator. A typical home in Korea has one standard fridge and another for *kimchi*, and many homes also have an extra one. The avarice is situated deep within the refrigerator, which causes us to believe that joy and happiness come from stocking the appliance full of various food items. If Nero took pleasure in enjoying everything that was readily available, we've taken a step further by filling up our desires in advance. This is why emptying the fridge is one of the ways we can reduce our gluttony and protect our health.

Conditions like high blood pressure, high cholesterol, diabetes, and gout can vastly improve or even resolve simply by changing one's diet. I firmly believe that reducing meat consumption even a little bit will improve both human health and the environment. The biggest culprits of dietary greed are meat and gluttony. Just as a clear crystal reflects a nearby object, humans can end up reflecting the nature of the animals we eat through traits like aggression, violence, impatience, and shamelessness. We bring about our own suffering because of our problematic diet.

Korea's long-held system of *ondol*[2] proves that we are a nation of farmers and gatherers. During the Goryeo Dynasty, meat was restricted by the Buddhist state. It began appearing on Korean dining tables again at the start of the Joseon Dynasty. Then, after the Korean War, the country was rapidly Westernized, and meat consumption expanded even further. But Korea's people carry a vegetarian gene. For example, people in the East have shorter legs because we have long intestines. If a Westerner's intestine is two meters long, an Easterner's is four and a half meters. So, although some Koreans say a meat-based diet is more filling, a lot more people say it makes them feel uncomfortable inside.

Through this ever-increasing consumption of animal proteins, we've compromised our respect for life and destroyed our ability to coexist and live in harmony with all beings. To achieve the best-marbled beef and pork, animals are crammed into tight spaces where it's hard to breathe. Often, the teeth of the young animals are removed because they may bite their too-close neighbors. Male chicks are killed by being suffocated in sacks, while the beaks of female chicks are cut off to prevent them from attacking others. Male animals are castrated to soften their meat, and most livestock are injected with antibiotics to prevent disease caused by their poor care. These optimally fattened livestock don't even reach full maturity before they're slaughtered and brought onto our tables. As described in Melanie Joy's book, *Why We Love Dogs, Eat Pigs, and Wear Cows*, humans

---

2 *Ondol* (온돌) is a floor heating system in traditional Korean architecture. Its usage dates back to prehistoric times.

have fallen into a carnivorous schema where we operate with dangerous numbness and do whatever we want with animals, suffocating their natures and shortening their lifespans. How will consuming their energies affect us? If we truly respect all life, we can't harm the life of a single ant or even a blade of grass—and those who don't harm others don't have to worry about developing the diseases brought on by gluttony.

People are starving worldwide, yet 30% of the earth's grains go toward feeding the livestock we consume at our tables. We could almost eradicate famine simply by reducing meat consumption to one-fifth of the current rate. For this reason, many religious organizations and schools have designated meatless days once a week.

Currently, 51% of the world's greenhouse gasses result from raising livestock, making meat consumption a pivotal environmental issue. The destruction of the environment in the North Pole, South Pole, and Amazon rainforest has resulted in an abnormal global climate and the destabilization of the earth's strata. Distancing ourselves from meat even slightly would enable humans, plants, and animals to breathe more peacefully. A world of happy coexistence is just within reach—one where we won't have to hear the sad sound of cowbells. All it takes is to eat less meat.

While a light diet is vital to soothing gluttony, this is not something you can simply change overnight. We all tend to fear what we find unfamiliar, which means it requires enormous courage to make any change we've set our mind to. Yet even things that seem difficult begin naturally when the time is right. It starts the moment we make up our minds. From there, we can continue to make significant changes by simply taking one step at a time.

Ultimately, transitioning to a lighter diet is a process of reducing desire, so it's best to look for ways to train the mind first. For instance, if you aren't used to preparing your own meals, it's crucial to experience buying tofu or cabbage for yourself. Ideally, we would all be able to stock our pantries at a bustling local marketplace full of fresh ingredients and lively sellers, but even a supermarket will suffice.

Picture this: you've bought yourself a small vegetable steamer, as well as some cabbage, tofu, and a bit of rice. Once home, you wash the cabbage thoroughly and place it in the steamer. Cutting the tofu in half, you blanch it slightly in a pot of boiling water on your stove. When the meal is ready, you place just enough tofu and cabbage to nourish yourself on a large plate. Add a spoonful of rice and two kinds of *banchan*[3] to the plate as well. Ladle stew or soup into a small bowl without pouring too much stock. Finally, look quietly at the food. Take a moment to think about where all this food came from, feeling gratitude. You may not experience the fullness of gratitude at first, but if you repeat this process every time you sit down to eat, eventually, a day will come when the ritual gives rise to it. Taste the food slowly as you scoop its scent into the bowl of your mind. By preparing each meal with this approach, one can begin to form a habit of temperance and find fulfillment in simple, natural food. Temple food isn't just a cuisine; it is the practice of forming a habit of eating with one's heart and mind.

---

3 *Banchan* (반찬): Korean side dish

If you find committing to a lighter diet difficult, you might try fasting—putting a daily pause on eating; engaging in the practice of resetting the mind and body. During a fast, you simply rest and empty yourself so that afterward, you feel realigned and experience the gratitude that naturally arises from practicing patience and self-control. However, fasting requires a strong will, so I advise against doing it merely because a friend recommended it or because you read about it in a book. There are multiple factors to watch out for, so beginners should get help from someone more experienced. Although there are many different ways to fast, most people usually consume only water or enzyme drinks. Not only does fasting give your internal organs a break from the constant work of digestion, but it also allows you to rest your eyes and head by taking a pause from books, screens, and other forms of distraction.

Before beginning a fast, it's best to prepare by abstaining from sizable portions of heavy food. If you have a cold, your body is tired, or you're getting ready for a big event, it's ill-advised to go on a fast. It's good to take an anthelmintic the day before beginning a fast and to get an enema on the first day. If the goal of the fast is dietary, prepare by consuming foods high in folic acid and avoiding greasy food.

Consider the following meal plan for preparing for a fast:

Breakfast - vegetable porridge with broccoli, carrots, shiitake mushrooms, ginkgo, and brown rice
Morning Snack – one-half a boiled tomato or one-quarter of an apple
Lunch - vegetables like cabbage and greens
Afternoon Snack - chew on two pieces of carrot for a long time
Dinner - one-quarter block of tofu and fruit juice

Fasting requires cutting out all food and beverages except water. However, during a fast, you can take in as much air as you wish. As you focus on your breath, you'll feel the purification taking place in your body. Observing the breath is an important complementary practice to fasting. Typically, most of us overlook the act of breathing as we go about our lives. But breath is the energy closest to our feelings. When we're tired, we release deep breaths. When we've gone through a difficult experience, we breathe a long sigh of relief. When we're happy, we take joyful breaths, matching our laughter. When we're sad, we take fast, rough breaths. Our breath is closely related to our lives, so I stress the importance of implementing a breathing practice during a fast.

It's not difficult to practice breathing. Just as one can perform small acts of abstinence from food before transitioning to an increasingly lighter diet, one can also begin breathwork by implementing small practices at first. Begin by lying down or sitting still for five to ten minutes twice or thrice daily to observe your breath. If this goes well, begin to draw attention to the lower belly, taking slow, deep breaths, then releasing them lightly.

Consider the following breathing practice for the lower abdomen:

Begin by focusing your attention three centimeters below your belly button. Inhale and then pause, holding your breath in the area of your attention.
Now, imagine your breath slowly leaving your body through your tailbone. Without exerting yourself, practice for about ten minutes. You should continue to breathe slowly to avoid breathlessness. If you get a headache, reduce the length of your breaths or your overall practice time—settle on what works best for you.

The Buddha reached nirvana through *Anapanasati*: the practice of observing the breath and noticing the feelings and sensations that arise. Even a simple breathing practice can offer tremendous insight, so it's essential to treat the breath carefully and practice mindful breathing. Even doing the exercise above for ten minutes requires quite a bit of patience. But once you're used to the practice, it becomes possible to breathe through the skin: not only do we breathe through the nose and mouth, but we also use our whole skin for breathing, vitalizing our metabolism, improving circulation, and invigorating the mind and body. This is why, for example, the practice of *poongyok*[4] is good for the body.

Similarly, a daily practice of mindful breathing also calms the mind and purifies the body. Once you become familiar with the practice, you'll gain confidence and enjoy it more easily. This practice also awakens us to the fact that arrogance and greed are useless, helping with attaining a lighter diet or the practice of fasting.

Fasting loosens muscles and eliminates toxins in the body. To make it even more effective, you can accompany a fasting practice with aerobic exercises like yoga to give you greater vitality. Consider drinking at least two liters of water a day as well. These kinds of activities give life to the intestines, form muscles, and help achieve bodily balance.

Overeating can lead to disease and harm one's mind and body. Of all the worldly desires, gluttony can be the cause of other types of greed. Because we live in a modern society with so many options for food, overcoming gluttony is an important practice. The habit of eating lightly before a fast

---

4 *Poongyok* (풍욕) is the practice of bathing in the wind by lying or sitting naked, covering up the body with a blanket or sheet, and repeating this step multiple times.

purifies the soul. This is why the Buddha emphasized eating lightly as a method of practice. Stepping through the doorway to a lighter diet is a clear sign that you are entering the path of more profound practice.

Jin (진): From Greed to Fear

After joining the temple, my days got busier. Most newly ordained monks study in Gangwon or practice in their meditation rooms. But because the elderly monk at my temple had passed away, I stayed in the temple to perform the one-hundred-day prayer multiple times and look after all the offerings. I was still a beginner and didn't know anything about Buddhism.

One hot summer day, I was busy carrying bricks, cement, and sand for plastering work; making jelly with acorns I picked up in the mountains; carrying bucketfuls of soaked beans down to the village mill to grind them; and kindling a fire for the cauldron to make tofu, all the while wiping away tears and reciting the Guan Yin prayer. Sweat streamed down my face as I listened to the sound of the *moktak*[5]; I kept repeating the prostrations for letting go. Despite my struggles, during this time, I also naturally began to spend more time in the kitchen, and my interest in temple food gradually started to grow. Unbeknownst to me, my two hands were thoroughly absorbing the tradition of temple food as I served the elder monks.

Then, suddenly, I was gripped by a series of illnesses, my body trapped like a spy caught in a security radar. I was suffering from hypothyroidism, which led to weight gain. On top of that, I slipped on a snowy road and got a herniated disk and sciatica. Other diseases showed signs of having soaked my body with their worldly energies as well. The nature of the

---

5 *Moktak* (목탁): a wooden gong used by monks in prayer

Buddha within was clouded by anxiety as discomfort and frustration took over. It was a karmic storm, the diseases brought on by a mind that hadn't yet conquered its demons. Fears passed on from childhood had created illness at long last, and I couldn't escape the thought that my choice to become a monk to leave behind a lonely and pitiful life was bringing me more pain than anything else. Despair and anguish surrounded me from all directions. My body was wrapped tightly in what the Buddha called suffering. Anxiety, nerves, tension, worries, loneliness, sadness, pain, suffering, and rage overtook me all at once.

To fight these fears, I recommitted to my spiritual practice. But as my illness improved, it took a long time for my body to recover fully. Weight gain was my biggest problem. No matter how hard I tried to devote myself to the cause, I couldn't lose weight. I'd had a habit of eating well since I was young and had also formed a habit of eating the leftover food after service at the temple, which made it difficult to fast. Since the temple didn't have a proper fridge, we had to gather and eat the leftover food before it spoiled. If we had wild greens, we seasoned them. If we had *jeon*[6] we put them in our stew. We didn't leave any waste. This reality led to overeating, and it was incredibly difficult to correct something that had so strongly taken root. So, I decided to go to Mount Jirisan.

I embarked on the path of Buddhist practice for the second time at a small cave resembling a decrepit storage house on a narrow, winding road. Committed to a 1,000-day prayer practice, I rose to recite prayers around the grounds each day at dawn, gathered herbs, stirred acorn jelly, made tofu and *doenjang*,[7] and performed offerings. I knew the cause of my

---

6 *Jeon* (전): Korean pancakes usually made with vegetables
7 *Doenjang* (된장): fermented soybean paste

suffering was internal, not external, and 1,000 days would ensure I could look within myself properly.

At the same time, I started building Guemsuam Temple. I joined a community organization protesting against building a dam on the mountain and learned about the sanctity of life. As I began honoring that sanctity, I started to find freedom from my sick body.

Considering my previous eating habits, I was unfamiliar with a light diet. But gradually, I began to let go of my fear of the unknown. I distanced myself from overeating as I grew familiar with fasting and eating lightly. People often ask those practicing a lighter or vegetarian diet, "How can you live on that? I'd die if I ate like that." They fail to think about how they're suffering from various ailments and slowly destroying their own healthy life by practicing the opposite. These people constantly crave food from a place of fear and anxiety, experiencing rage, hostility, and ill will if they can't fill their stomachs, which is then expressed in their behavior toward others. It's only natural that one would get sick. When one is sick inside, the body suffers outwardly as well. Mind and body are bound together in disease.

Among my students, there are men of all ages. One is in his fifties and tends to clash with the other students. You could say he's successful and holds a stable position in society, yet he was prone to anger whenever things didn't go his way. At last, it reached a point where the other students would avoid being on his team or sitting next to him in class.

While he seemed to regret the whole situation, the clashes continued.

His diet consisted of alcohol, meat, garlic, and things that generate a lot of energy. His complexion was always dark or flushed, giving him the appearance of being impatient and prone to anger. So, I pulled him aside and advised him to switch to a vegetarian diet to balance his temperament and avoid damaging his heart. I also scolded him sincerely for living in a state of anger so severe it was bound to bring about an explosion in his blood vessels or the heart. Six months after I advised him, he came to me with glee, saying he was beginning to see how to approach his life differently. He said that eating temple food made him feel comfortable in both mind and body, smiling like an innocent child as he informed me that he'd even begun seeking vegetarian food on his business trips abroad. His dark red complexion, which seemed to have come straight out of a smelting furnace, had changed to the clear pink of a peach blossom.

Gluttony can give birth to fear if it seems we won't attain what we want. It can generate anger if we become anxious. When we reach for food out of fear and anger, we might eat without care, causing us to suffer disease or weight gain. Suddenly, we find ourselves trapped in a cycle of fear, anger, and illness.

All the earth's bounty belongs to us—if we only take what is necessary. Just as we needn't be greedy for the sun and the moon to give us their light, we can trust that everything we need is within us. All of existence lives inside the power of positive faith. There's no reason to fear, worry, or feel angry when we can't fulfill our desires. Just as I arrived at the peace and abundance of Mount Jirisan to pray with a beginner's mind, we can renew our approach to consumption and begin our relationship to eating again. If we simply observe, show compassion, and practice understanding, we can peel away any layers of fear and invite a new reality onto our tables and into our hearts. Our minds can continue to expand as we realize that harmony is the source of mercy, compassion, and awakening. When fear, anger, and malice disappear, we will discover that infinite compassion is the only thing truly embracing us. Right from that moment, we will lift our spoons with renewed hearts.

Chi (치): The Trap of Ignorance

Ignorance is the fertilizer that grows greed, fear, and anger—negative emotions that come from mistaking what is fake for what is real. This delusion confuses a false self with the real one and gives rise to all negative thoughts and feelings.

One day, I received a visitor who wanted her pregnant teenage daughter to stay at the temple. Her face was burnt as black as her worrisome heart. This mother said she had advised her daughter to get an abortion but that her daughter insisted on raising the child despite having no means to do so and begged me to convince her otherwise. I took a deep breath and began watching the daughter.

For several days, I felt sadness as I saw how her actions had rippled into this moment. We all carry duality, like two sides of a coin, and this young girl seemed to be living on the side of negativity. I could see that deep within her, she was clinging to the false beliefs that living a life true to herself meant coyly deceiving others, making light of grave situations, and not looking after her body. She thought she would be happy if only she could be with her boyfriend. At the tender age of sixteen, she had grown to rely solely on her senses—full of worldly desires. All her attention was focused on obscene content, extravagant appearances, and tasty foods. Of all her uncontrolled cravings, her desire for male attention had made the most significant impact, obscuring her ability to distinguish right from wrong and manifesting outwardly as selfishness. The patterns of her life that were consuming her had come from ignorance. How many of the 8,000 lives the Buddha spoke of had she lived without a mate? Perhaps the habit of chasing after sex had followed her from the last life into this one, as naturally as the fact of one seeking out food when hungry.

Subconscious desires that lurk beneath our outer lives like an iceberg underwater tend to trap us inside powerful animalistic desires. Today, marriage is viewed as being appropriate only after one comes of age. But during the Joseon Dynasty, getting married before the age of fifteen was customary. So, one could say that this girl was merely following a different societal pattern. Maybe she just couldn't accept the contemporary idea that choosing a mate is best after graduating college, joining society, and dating several people. Although her boyfriend had fled the responsibility of raising their child, perhaps it was only natural for her to want to have a child in his likeness, whether out of love or repentance—just as it was equally natural for her mother to consider the whole affair a misfortune.

The law of cause and effect means foolish actions give way to predictably imprudent results. When we make unwise choices, we face proportionally unfortunate consequences. The sooner we awaken to this reality and build wisdom, the faster we'll be released from making difficult choices that result in despair. It's possible to escape the cycle of desire, no matter how deeply entrenched in it one has been.

Sometimes, this ignorance and delusion manifests as a craving for food. Other times, it shows up as a desire for wealth or success. No matter how such errors in judgment appear, they cloud our eyes and ears to wisdom and lead us down the wrong path. If we gain the insight to eradicate the cause of our suffering, we can prevent more suffering in the future. But for the most part, humans tend to choose thorny paths by following familiar patterns and end up in tears, just like this teenage girl.

The consequences of ignorance emerge like flies from rotting fruit. Societal folly makes us all suffer. For example, recently, I learned that an accident at the Incheon Subway construction site caused the road to sink twenty meters. Although local residents and workers at the site voiced concern for their safety, the police, city officials, and experts all appeared to be concerned only with deflecting fault and shifting blame. Rather than addressing the issue, they played hide-and-seek with the cause of the accident, analyzing safety concerns and revamping the whole operation. When you don't see things through the lens of wisdom and insight, you only see what's right in front of you—as though you're shrouded in a dark veil of ignorance. How can you expect to avoid an earthquake when you're shoveling dirt from one area to fill up the ocean?

The meals we consume are no exception. Every day, we fill our dinner tables so haphazardly we can't even tell what ingredients are used. We've become used to serving fast and pre-made food out of convenience. But the most unwise foods to consume are genetically modified organisms— the artificial combinations that become GMOs. Although some say that GMOs are the solution to global food supply issues, their development will boomerang back to us as the key culprit in environmental destruction. The most GMO-affected crop is beans. Korea's native beans are small, scrumptious, and have a sheen—a variety that has been cultivated since the formation of the ancient Balhae and Goryeo after the Gojoseon Kingdom,[8] when the arrival of Buddhism brought food practices centered

---

8 Gojoseon was the first ancient kingdom of Korean people; its founding commonly cited as 2333 BCE by the mythological figure, Dangun.

around beans. As such, beans are inseparable
from the Korean people as a crop that has
been around for ages. If you make *doenjang*
with them, they're tasty and highly nutritious.
During the Three Kingdoms era, it was said that
fermented soybeans were included as part of the
gift offerings when candidates for queen entered
the palace. It has also been noted that the people

of ancient Goguryeo were so skilled at fermenting food that their *doenjang*
was well known.

It's a sad state of affairs that these beans are getting genetically modified
and turned into soybean milk, bean sprouts, and tofu. *Doenjang* and
ganjang are the essential ingredients of Korean food and cannot be
made without beans. It's horrifying to think that these staples are being
genetically modified. People who take issue with livestock feed and
replace cows' milk with soybean milk aren't safe either. How foolish is it
to give livestock the same genetically modified foods that we ourselves
eat? The stupidity of feeding livestock with a mixture of GMOs, animal
byproducts, and pesticides can only result in catastrophe.

That's not all. Many dangers await us at the table. While plants grown
in a healthy environment give us good energy in return, it's evident
that anything produced in a polluted environment will eventually lead
to sickness. All this energy gets recycled back into nature. Our unwise
desire to buy big, colorful produce rather than those nibbled by insects,
combined with the corporate pursuit of profit by selling ingredients grown
en masse, can have a detrimental effect.

There's yet another type of ignorance atop the table: food additives. Preservatives, sterilizers, antioxidants, coloring, bleaching agents, condiments, acidulants, sweeteners, flavoring, fortifying nutrients, flour improvers, emulsifiers, thickeners, gelling and coating agents, leaveners, defoamers, extractors, and liquid paraffin are only a few. In fact, it's difficult to find products *without* any additives. Do we really believe we won't have problems storing all this inside our bodies?

Greed, desire, worry, fear, and rage are all born of this ignorance—placing humanity on a trajectory that shatters peace for ourselves, our families, our neighbors, and the earth. It is imprudent to proudly wear leather shoes made from calves that were killed within two hours of birth; to carry wallets made from teeth violently plucked from stingrays' mouths because they're believed to bring wealth; to consume juicy, marbled pork from antibiotic-injected pigs raised in cramped cages. These are the fruits of foolishness that wilt life. However, in the light of wisdom, such errors can melt away like snow in the spring sunshine.

We must think about the foundations upon which we're building our lives. Although our feet are one of the most overlooked parts of our body, everyone knows how important they are. Similarly, how important must the land be on which all life depends? The word "land" is often used when engaging with fundamental principles. This is because land is the foundation of all things. Yet, our farmlands are polluted with pesticides, chemical fertilizers, and antibiotics. The earth is suffering due to our desire to grow more attractive produce en masse. Can we really retain our health when we're consuming produce from diseased land?

Spring gives birth to life. Upon its arrival, the land is plowed and seeds planted. But before plowing, we need to remove any plastic sheeting that has covered the ground through winter. Even if you don't use pesticides or chemical fertilizers, failing to manage plastic coverings can emit EDCs (endocrine-disrupting chemicals). No matter how much I clean up my space, there seems to be no end to the plastic thrown away by the women who planted chilis last spring. I've even spotted sheets of plastic caught atop tree branches. When plastic gets heated, it produces EDCs that can cause endocrine disorders when absorbed. These hormonal disorders poison our lymph nodes, as evidenced by the rise in breast and prostate cancer in modern society. In fact, plastic is often used in all seasons to gather crops, but it's best to avoid using it or take proper care if it's used.

In contrast, the land in front of our temple is made of healthy soil that's been organic for the last twenty years. To keep the soil healthy, we must weed the earth and give it organic manure instead of pesticide-treated fertilizer. To prevent acidification—which occurs when soil is overused and overtreated, grows old and sick, and loses vitality and immunity, making it difficult to grow healthy plants—we must love the land and not be greedy. Once acidification occurs, if chemicals are used to force growth, the land becomes even weaker and thrust into a negative cycle of constant depletion. The EU now has strict bans and regulations placed on pesticides. Korea also needs a system to control their use. Currently, we're acting like we're taking medicine to prevent cancer, using pesticides out of habit and the sense that others are doing so as well. But if we keep using pesticides and chemical fertilizers at will, it will soon become more surprising if we *don't* get sick.

Over time, the local elders living near our temple all passed away from cancer, the result of spending their whole lives using pesticides. Throughout their lives, it seemed they each took turns spraying herbicides and insecticides at frequent intervals. The man who lived next door used to cause a ruckus by spraying herbicides whenever grass grew on the road behind the temple, calling it an inconvenience. I had to beg him to stop in as warm a tone as possible, telling him the chemical would pool in our front yard whenever it rained.

We must do whatever it takes to protect the land that is getting sick before our very eyes, never ceasing to do our part personally to create a healthy earth. Before we spray the land with pesticides to grow more crops, we must first grow a healthy mindset. We must practice letting go of greed and observing our hearts, planting seeds within ourselves of promise not to harm the land.

Even when our unhealthy desires seem to have vanished, we carry seeds that have not yet sprouted as long as ignorance remains. Even a small, unwise impulse can make such a seed bloom. Though greed, fear, and rage may cease, sometimes we still can't see the light of wisdom due to that last remaining speck of ignorance—a poison that clouds a righteous mind and leads us down an imprudent path. Yet, if we step closer to the wisdom that lies on the opposite side of ignorance, we will discover a light that dispels this darkness. We can all live free and healthy lives with healed hearts and minds.

***

One bright, sunny day, a twenty-five-year-old woman suffering from eczema visited the temple. Although she was pretty, brilliant, and skilled in foreign languages, she had social phobia due to her condition. She left a trail of white skin flakes she constantly needed to sweep up wherever she went. It was painful to see her carry a broom at all times, like a disciple of Jainism.

After she started fasting, she began showing minor improvements. But later in her fasting regimen, after reintroducing fruit into her diet, she ate half a watermelon. I was away during this time, and the young woman lamented that I hadn't instructed her on how much she could eat. She'd also heard it was permissible to drink a bit of tea, so she drank some robust black herbal tea, thinking it would be more effective than taking enzymes or fermented tea. Her determination to cure disease by cutting off food had lay dormant as a not-yet-sprouted seed of foolishness, leading her to thoughts like, *Watermelon is the same as water. I can eat as much as I want. It's just fruit anyway, not flour or carbs,* and *I've been starving. I've lost a lot of weight. Tea is fine to consume, so taking some potent black tea with medicinal herbs is probably best.* These whispers of her mind had tempted her, and as a result, her poor, weak body suffered a stomachache.

The biggest problem with this kind of error in judgment is that it continues to snowball. If one attempts to recover from a fast by eating meat or other heavy foods immediately, the positive effects of fasting won't be realized. A foolish mind is like the illusion of the moon reflected on moving waters: it may seem as if the moon is flowing with the tide or its light is coming from the water itself, but this is a delusion that can plunge one into chaos.

After this incident, the young woman never repeated the same mistake. The uncomfortable experience made her reflect on herself as she swept the floor. She grew slow to act and keen on observing within. Slow observance is the first step to discern whether we need something or if our mind merely tells us we need it. Ask yourself: are you doing something out of self-love or simply a temptation to calm your mind? Are you attempting to relieve anxiety, or are you trying to fulfill a desire? The young woman began to clearly discern these differences just by observing. Once she recognized the darkness of ignorance, she stopped repeating the same mistakes—and even if she did, she would now catch herself in them. She had discovered wisdom through the simple act of observation. With this discovery, she could walk joyfully in the bright light of day. She no longer needed the broom. All she needed was her bright smile.

Mung Bean Jelly Salad with Bamboo Shoots

(Juksoon Tangpyeongchae)

Bamboo shoots sprout with the energy of a cool early morning. After giving themselves to be consumed as food, they sprout again in a few days, offering themselves again with morning dew. They are different from the human mind that keeps wanting more after consuming so much. Bamboo teaches the lesson of stepping out of the shadow of greed.

Ingredients

18 ounces bamboo shoots

8 ounces *cheongpo muk*[1] (mung bean jelly)

4 shiitake mushrooms

½ carrot

½ cucumber

1 ounce *seogi beoseot* (rock tripe mushroom/lichens) or *mogi beoseot* (wood ear mushrooms)

Sesame oil, salt, *gukganjang* (soup soy sauce) for seasoning

For prepping bamboo shoots:

Water from rinsing rice; if you don't have rice water, then dilute some flour in water as a substitute

½ tablespoon *doenjang*

---

1 *Cheongpo muk* (mung bean jelly) is a savory jelly-like block made by boiling mung bean starch in water and cooling. You can find mung bean starch and, sometimes, pre-made mung bean jelly in Korean markets.

Sweet vinegar for cucumber:

¼ cup white vinegar

2 tablespoons sugar

½ tablespoon salt

Pine nut dressing:

3 tablespoons finely minced pine nuts

½ tablespoon *gyeoja* (hot mustard)

½ tablespoon white vinegar

3 tablespoons pear juice

Directions

1. Slice the bamboo shoots lengthwise and peel the skin. In a pot, combine the rice water with *doenjang* and boil the bamboo shoots over high heat for about 20 minutes to remove the bitter-sour taste. Rinse in cold water and drain.

2. Julienne the bamboo shoots and pan-fry lightly in sesame oil with a pinch of salt.

3. Julienne the mung bean jelly into pieces about 3 inches long and ⅓-inch thick. Blanch briefly in boiling water, then lightly season with salt and sesame oil.

4. Cut the shiitake mushrooms into thin strips, then season lightly with soup soy sauce and sesame oil, and pan-fry briefly.

5. Julienne the carrot, then pan-fry in sesame oil with a pinch of salt.

6. Prepare the sweet vinegar by mixing together the vinegar, sugar, and salt. Slice the cucumber into thin sheets, discarding the seedy part, and julienne. Marinate it lightly in the sweet vinegar.

7. Dust off debris and remove the hard stem from the rock tripe mushrooms, then season with soup soy sauce and sesame oil, and pan-fry.

8. Combine the pine nut dressing ingredients in a separate bowl and mix well.

9. Arrange the prepared mung bean jelly and vegetables on a platter and serve with the pine nut dressing.

Squash & *Dureup* Rollups

(Danhobak Dureup Jeonbyeong)

Anger is the heat that arises from our bodies when things don't go our way. It can be controlled with a healthy balancing recipe like this one. These rollups are made with one of the most popular Korean spring wild vegetables, *dureup* (angelica tree) shoots. The colorful ingredients are nicely wrapped in a thin, crepe-like pancake.

Ingredient

10 *dureup* (angelica tree) shoots or asparagus tips

2 ounces *danhobak* (kabocha squash)

1 cup all-purpose flour

2 tablespoons crushed perilla seeds or sesame seeds

1 tablespoon potato starch or cornstarch

Gukganjang (soup soy sauce), sesame oil, sesame seeds for seasoning

Oil for pan frying (mix 2 tablespoons each cooking oil and perilla seed oil, or simply use cooking oil)

Directions

1. Blanch the *dureup* in salted boiling water, then rinse in cold water and tightly squeeze out excess water. Then season lightly with the soup soy sauce, sesame oil, and sesame seeds.
2. Remove the skin and seeds of the squash. Using a peeler, make thin slices, then stack them up and cut into thin matchsticks.

3. Sift the all-purpose flour, perilla seeds, and potato starch together. Add water, starting with a cup and adding more as needed to achieve a thin batter consistency similar to that of crepes. Season with the soup soy sauce. You can add green tea powder, beet powder, and other berry powder/juice to color the batter.

4. Heat a small amount of oil in a non-stick pan over medium heat. Pour a spoonful of the batter onto the pan and spread it out three to four times, using the back of the spoon, into a palm-sized thin, round pancake. Cook until the edges are slightly dry, about 30 seconds per side. Repeat with the remaining batter.

5. Place the squash and *dureup* on a pancake and roll it up. Since the ingredients are already seasoned, no sauce may be needed on the side.

Potato Noodles

(Gamja Guksu)

Foolishness lingers, but wisdom eventually prevails. This is because both brightness and darkness coexist in our own hearts. Raw potato soaked in cold water for a long time to remove the starch brings out an unexpected texture and flavor.

Ingredients

1 large white potato

1 cup green peas

½ teaspoon salt

1 cup water

Garnish:

2 cherry tomatoes, halved

Black sesame seeds

Directions

1. Peel the potato and cut it into long and thin matchsticks. Rinse several times and further remove the starch by soaking the potato in cold water while preparing the peas. Change the water once or twice while soaking.

2. Cook the peas in boiling water with salt to keep the green color bright.

3. Drain and rinse the peas in cold water, and then puree in a blender with 1 cup of water.

4. Drain the raw potato noodles, mound them in a bowl, and pour the cold pea soup over.

5. Garnish with the cherry tomatoes and a pinch of black sesame seeds.

part two

A Table of
Wisdom

The Japanese Zen Buddhist monk Dōgen Zenji left detailed descriptions of how monks approach cooking in his book *Tenzo Kyōkun*.[1] This book does not merely discuss food but also conveys the principle that everything in daily life is a practice. Cooking is no exception. *Tenzo Kyōkun* emphasizes the importance of cooking each ingredient with care and honoring its natural taste. Dōgen simplifies one's approach to cooking by citing three mindsets and three virtues.

The first of the three mindsets is that of a joyful heart (희심), particularly the joy of making and serving food. Dōgen instructs readers to approach cooking as a practice of delight, which enables the making of food with wholeheartedness.

The second mindset is that of a nurturing heart (노심), or the practice of paying attention to the most minor details. In other words, one must cook with the loving heart of a parent, considering the person who will eat the food rather than cooking simply for oneself.

The third mindset is that of a big heart (대심), or the ability to maintain balance like the mountains and oceans instead of getting swept up in pettiness. This speaks to letting go of obsession, remaining faithful to universal truths, and cooking honestly with depth and scale.

Cooking requires the proper virtues as well as the right mindsets. The three virtues are purity (청결함/청절), tenderness (부드러움/유연), and naturality (법다움/여법). Preparing a beautiful meal with all of one's heart from beginning to end is a mindful practice if embodied with these three mindsets and virtues. I lament our current state of affairs, which

---

1 *Tenzo Kyōkun* (전좌교운): a 13th-century essay entitled *Instructions for the Cook*

requires me to point this out amidst the ignorance of laziness, bias, and selfishness. I hope that if we realize these truths and overcome our follies one by one, we can each set a table of wisdom.

Some give alms at the temple by making food and performing other chores. When you observe those who prepare the meals, you can feel how much care goes into the food. Even if you only visit the temple on a holiday—like the day of Buddha's birth—to eat some *bibimbap*, you'll witness the character of these chefs. These practitioners understand that when you make offerings to the Buddha, you must select the best grains with care, serve rice while wearing a protective mask, and slice *kimchi* neatly in accordance with its nature. The almsgiver also serves the monks as they would serve the Buddha by making food that assists their meditation. They serve the practicing Buddhists in the same way. To make a joyful meal at home or at a restaurant, cook like these almsgivers with the heart of a parent—a glad and generous heart—and remember the three virtues of purity, tenderness, and naturality.

The Three Virtues of Food

Purity (청정)

Pure innocence, a peaceful heart, chastity, cleanliness, purification. These are the qualities of the most elegant and tasteful food and what make up the virtue of purity. Such purity comes from an innocence unmarred by any external influences. That's why I always visit the temple on Mount Jirisan at least once a week, no matter how busy I am at the Temple Food Center in Seoul, where I also keep up my practice and meditation.

A sincere heart forms the basis of cooking in accordance with the nature of each ingredient. It's best to use ingredients grown in clean soil, water, sunlight, and air. We must always embody gratitude when seeking ingredients and maintain cleanliness while interacting with them. As long as we remain grateful for the entire process of gathering or purchasing the components of a meal, we can produce dishes that bear this purity of heart.

The process of cooking is equally important. We must treat the ingredients carefully and neatly manage the plates that hold them. To maintain purity, we must take care throughout the process, from preparing the ingredients to cooking them with peaceful sincerity. Lighter herbs must be washed, blanched, and rinsed delicately—otherwise, they lose all their natural scent and flavor if you boil them unwashed before rinsing, instead of washing and blanching them. If this happens, it is common for a chef to start a vicious cycle of seasoning the now-bland greens with additives like sugar, salt, and sesame oil. We may still be able to make these mishandled ingredients taste good, but it's not beneficial to our health.

Last spring, I foraged some wild mountain greens to give to a visitor from Seoul. My visitor told me that while she loved the final dish, she found the entire process of preparing, washing, and cooking bothersome. My face reddened in front of those spring greens as I felt like I had tried to share something positive and produced a burden instead. I started preparing and cooking the greens immediately, realizing that had I given them away, she would have only stored them in the fridge for a while before throwing them out, perhaps feeling guilty for doing so. I apologized to the plants and cooked them with a thankful heart. This is how we must approach food: while maintaining a cleanliness of mind, body, and spirit from start to finish to preserve its virtue of purity.

Tenderness (유연)

If our bodies are flexible, we can be comfortable in all postures. If our food is tender, we can consume it more easily. Tender food is easy to digest, release, and circulate back into nature, where it is then brought to life again as healthy produce. The virtue of tenderness breathes life into the ecosystem. Straying from this virtue cannot give us healthy food.

For example, when you fry *naengi*[2] you must prepare them according to their shape. If you neglect this step out of laziness and just fry them all together, they won't cook evenly, making them difficult to eat. Likewise,

---

2 *Naengi* (냉이): shepherd's purse shoots, a fragrant green common in Korean cuisine, often eaten from the root to the leaves

when you grind mung beans to make pancakes, using the proper amount of water is essential to preventing them from becoming too tough. Making pancakes with peas is the same: if the dough is too runny, it will lose its starchiness and shape. Food handled without proper care and consideration cannot be said to contain the virtue of tenderness. Understanding the properties of mung beans allows us to cook delicious pancakes that are easy to digest, as is the case with all things in creation.

The virtue of tenderness teaches us to understand the characteristics of each ingredient and cook with care. Only in doing so can we make seasonal food appropriate for each diner's character, constitution, health, profession, and other aspects. When we eat food that has been prepared with tenderness, it produces saliva under the tongue, which aids digestion. Tenderness is an essential virtue for preparing food that is not too stimulating and soft enough to chew and digest easily.

Naturality (여법)

Naturality is the virtue that honors the inherent nature of each ingredient: rice as rice, soup as soup, and vegetables as vegetables. It also respects each cooking method, whether frying, steaming, roasting, or another. It's the virtue of eating organic food that enables us to live a healthy life.

I have an old friend from my school days who'd gather a group of our peers together to give us witty lectures on weird cooking methods, often recounting various episodes of her older sister's cooking in hilarious detail. One day, as she told it, my friend's sister made *sujebi*[3] by stirring together water and flour and then forming the dough with chopsticks.

---

3 *Sujebi* (수제비): a soup with hand-torn flour dumplings

My friend said it was the first time she'd seen such oddly shaped flour dumplings, and we laughed when she declared it a rare opportunity to eat such a dish. How was it possible to form the dough into dumplings using only chopsticks? And how funny the shapes must have looked!

She told of another time when her sister attempted to make a noodle soup by dumping all the dried noodles into boiling water at once, making them stick together, par cooked. She complained that the noodles were incredibly difficult to eat because they stuck together and did not separate even when stirred with chopsticks. Apparently, her sister only needed scissors and basic cutlery to cook—no need for a knife or cutting board when she'd had her hands or scissors. She used cutlery to fry and flip all kinds of food, often mixing all the ingredients together at once. She also found no need to set the table since they'd simply take out the plastic containers of *banchan*. They also didn't use a dishcloth; they merely wiped the table with a tissue between meals.

When you cook, each process must be natural. The ingredients themselves should be organic, and the methods of gathering, washing, cutting, and preparing them should be unaffected. At times, it's necessary to cook for the sake of convenience, but it's problematic to always prioritize the ease of convenience. My friend's sister just wanted cooking to be easy and expedient. She didn't understand the nature of her ingredients or treat them with gratitude. She cooked food with haste simply to fill an empty stomach, not with care and consideration for herself or her family.

When I ran into this friend recently at a cooking class, she informed me with her usual laughter, "My sister no longer makes strange foods. She earned her Korean and Western cooking licenses and changed completely. She now uses all kinds of tools and cooks properly with fresh ingredients." I laughed along with her. Her sister had lived in a world of ignorance before learning to cook. Now, she was living in a world of wisdom. Natural food is essential. Its virtue goes beyond cooking and enables us to live a life full of harmony.

How to Use Fire, Water, and Knives per Their Nature

All vegetables contain medicinal properties in their roots, stems, leaves, fruits, and flowers. The grains and beans that enter our bodies also interact positively with their systems. Since certain foods contain medicinal properties, they can be beneficial ingredients if we understand them. But misusing them can result in fatal harm. There's much to consider in cooking natural and harmonious food in which the ingredients complement the cooking process.

First, a cook must understand the traits of each ingredient and discern its most appropriate cooking method. One must also consider the mind and body of those we're serving. Even if we provide a healthy dish, it can still be harmful if the body isn't ready to receive it. For a newborn, the best food is milk from the mother's breast. As a child grows, we give them weaning foods in accordance with their stages of growth. Likewise, we must provide soft, easily absorbed foods for people whose bodies are weak so they can digest adequately and recover gradually.

Another area of caution to pay attention to while cooking is the use of fire, water, and knives. Food is made through a series of molecular processes; the most significant factor that influences the energy of ingredients is fire. If a cook can't control fire, they may burn or undercook their food, harming the positive energies of each component of their dish. Say we're making fresh *bibimbap* with spinach, shiitake mushrooms, carrots, and bean sprouts. It's important to blanch the bean sprouts lightly to maintain their crunchiness. In temple cuisine, we don't stir-fry raw vegetables in oil immediately because it affects their coloring and toughens the fiber. For example, in the case of bean sprouts, first, put sesame oil, water, and salt in a pan. Once this boils, add the bean sprouts. Cover with a lid until the sprouts become fragrant. This is how you prepare *bibimbap* with crunchy bean sprouts and greens.

Managing cooking water is important as well. Water comes from the circulation of rain absorbed by the earth, rising again as steam into the atmosphere. So, we must understand the preciousness of water before we start cooking. Mindful cooking begins from the moment we turn on the faucet, where we must pay attention to how we wash each ingredient. Leafy greens, for example, are best washed in a bowl of water or water run at a low pressure, as a high water pressure can damage the leaves. Aggressive washing harms the leaves, robs them of health, and releases the energy of fear and shock. One also must take particular care when washing raw mushrooms. If you soak them in water, they absorb it like a sponge and lose their natural flavor. Instead, it's best to rinse them quickly in your hands. Root vegetables should be washed in a bowl and rinsed quickly under running water.

When cooking with water, adjusting moisture levels after boiling is also essential. Too much moisture in noodles softens their chewy texture. Greens should be dried with a towel after boiling to maintain their freshness. Dipping them in *gochujang* while still damp can make them mushy or bland. If you pickle vegetables with too much moisture, it can get spoiled. It's crucial to control the water.

It's also important to prepare your ingredients for easy cooking and consumption. Light leafy greens should be handled gently by hand or knife. Too sharp knives can damage ingredients and make them lose their flavor. Using knives without care can also rapidly weaken an ingredient's natural properties or produce toxins. Ingredients that are shocked by the touch of a knife can taste rough or bitter as they try to protect themselves. We must carefully manage our knives as part of the cooking process.

Six Tastes and Six Intentions

The Chinese Buddhist monk Changlu Zongze wrote in the *Chanyuan Qinggui*,[4] "If the six tastes are not suitable and the food lacks three virtues, the tenzo's offering is incomplete."

This speaks to the principle that those who cook must maintain the three virtues and six flavors of food: bitter, sweet, salty, bland, sour, and spicy. Dōgen Zenji spoke about replacing bitterness and blandness with acerbity to cook according to the five tastes (sweet, spicy, sour, acerbic, salty), five colors (red, white, green, yellow, black), and five methods (raw, boiled, roasted, fried, steamed). Of the six flavors, blandness preserves the natural taste of the ingredients. Let's explore the six tastes in more detail.

It is said that bitter food is good for you. Indeed, bitterness has the brilliant capacity to restore vitality. Those with a weak heart or stomach can benefit from eating bitter foods like sorghum, lettuce, and mugwort. Mugwort has such tenacity that it was the first plant to sprout after the Hiroshima bombing. Motherwort helps with menstruation, infertility, and heatstroke.

The sweet flavors of fruits and vegetables refresh our mood, restore our taste buds, and assist with digestion. There's an Indian proverb that goes, "Sell your house to eat a durian." The fruit's taste is that tempting. The sweetness of foods like arrowroot, pumpkin, cabbage, and sweet potato

---

4 *The Rules of Purity in the Chan Monastery* (1103).

tastes good and benefits our health. In contrast, the false sweetness in fast food and instant meals has devastating effects on our bodies.

Foods with a naturally salty taste can have a beneficial effect on our kidneys because the rich minerals help to release blockages. While too much salt can cause illness, foods like black beans, glasswort, seaweed, kelp, hijiki, bamboo salt, *doenjang*, and soy sauce all taste of salt and help with obesity and constipation.

Blandness is a necessary quality that preserves the natural taste of each ingredient. Too much seasoning conceals an ingredient's authentic flavor, so we must take care not to overwhelm the simple, natural, and bland tastes of these foods. Diners often say that bland food doesn't "taste good," but this is an erroneous statement since blandness is one of many tastes.

We often salivate or close our eyes when we imagine a sour taste. Sourness benefits the liver, eyesight, and digestion. It can also help boost appetite. Sour fruits and other ingredients commonly used in temple cuisine include *omija* (five-flavor or schisandra berries), Cornelian cherries, blackberries, and pomegranate rinds. Again, we must exercise caution with these, as too much sourness can disrupt the gastrointestinal system.

Spiciness is effective for stress relief, blood circulation, the release of digestive fluids, and weight loss. When trying to lose weight, it is best to restrict salt intake and limit sweet sauces, so spices like *gochugaru* (Korean chili powder) mustard, or wasabi can add more flavor to food. Leafy greens like summer radish, celery, and brown mustard can also taste spicy. These greens are well complemented with a sauce made from mustard, perilla seeds, and *maesilcheong* (green plum syrup). Chili pepper can also be added to sweet vegetables like cabbage and rolled up with rice to create an enjoyable meal.

Eating slowly as you savor these six tastes is a good habit. Eat with your eyes first, then your hands, and your mouth. Feel the ingredient's texture, its softness as it passes your throat, the fullness in your belly, and the satisfaction in your heart. Eating slowly like this lets you enjoy your food and experience all six tastes.

The first of the six intentions of the heart is "providing for others without producing waste (남에게 은혜를 베풀되 낭비하지 않음)." It's the heart of abundance that doesn't overflow when we cook, eat, and serve food. The second is "making an effort without blame (수고하되 원망하지 않음)." This describes the intention of sharing food with care and effort without blaming the ingredients, taste, or people for their outcome. The third is the intention of "desire without greed (욕심을 가지되 탐내지 않음)," or having a passion for making tasty food without greed. The fourth is "remaining composed yet not proud (태연하되 교만하지 않음)," or being generous and abundant in all situations, which gives one a natural dignity that makes others look up to them. The fifth intention is "wielding power without being unruly (위세가 있되 사납지 않음)." This means commanding a presence is crucial without being too forceful or making others feel small. The final intention is "freedom without self-indulgence (자유롭되 방종하지 않음)," which means embracing the first five of these virtues without being confined by them. It's the beauty of using one's mind and body as lightly as a feather to allow both oneself and others to experience freedom with ease and flexibility.

These are the six beautiful Buddhist intentions of the heart.

The Four Elements of Temple Food

Human beings live as one breath with nature. As the Buddha said, each person's body is like a country. We carry life in our bodies, each one its own gigantic universe composed of the four elements: earth, water, fire, and wind. Like the *Flower Garland Sutra*'s "all within one and one within all," the four elements have an organic relationship with one another. In Buddhism, we say that everything is part of a whole. We are connected to everything around us and are one with nature. That's why we can't think about anything in separation from the whole.

Earth/Land (지)

Earth is a symbol of strength, groundedness, and bounty. Plants can't grow without the earth, and humans can't live without it. The land absorbs rain from the sky, water from pipes, and all other waste matter while constantly working to heal itself. If the land is healthy, so are plants. Then, the humans and animals who eat those vibrant plants are also healthy. When we take in this earth's energy, our bodies become strong of frame and build.

Minerals from the earth are contained in the waters, and the energy of those minerals benefits our bones. When our bodies are strong, our minds aren't easily shaken. The earth raises us with solid determination. Therefore, we must carefully return our waste back to the planet in a way that doesn't pollute so that it continues to circulate and purify. Our duty is to return less polluted matter to the earth—a symbol of ultimate tolerance.

The earth changes according to the seasons. It sprouts green spring leaves to replenish the land and grows weeds to protect the summer heat from reflecting back into space. The land is full of fruit in the fall and returns to an empty state in the winter to build fortitude in the cold.

Water (수)

Water flows calmly and coolly, placid enough to lay down life's oars. Like the oceans surrounding the land, water makes up 70% of our body. It is released through urine, stool, and sweat. This cycle is vital since blood, tears, nasal discharge, and other fluids are composed of water.

Except for those who suffer from edema, most people need around two liters of water a day. Water is necessary for making blood, and it's best to drink a lot of water after six o'clock in the evening because mornings have yang energy and evenings have yin energy. Drinking plenty of water for three months improves hematosis and makes skin glow since moisture facilitates lubrication.

We must consider whole-body circulation. Just as pooled water becomes stale and polluted, our bodies require regular replenishment with fresh water to retain vitality. Drinking fresh water that isn't too cold, hot, or salty is best. In cooking, you can't make dough without water. We must keep in mind the qualities of pliability and harmony in water.

Water changes form with the seasons. In the spring, it sparkles as dew. In the summer, it soaks the earth as rain. In the fall, it shines as raindrops with sunlight as its companion. In the winter, it covers the ground as cold snow. When the water gets polluted, the functions of our bodies do, too.

The water beneath the ground rises to the sky and turns into rain. The rain passes into the earth and becomes a spring—a source of drinking water. Water enters the bloodstreams of all living beings through osmosis. Just imagine how terrible it would be if it entered our veins without undergoing any kind of filtration process. Water is the basic lubricant of life, making it the most necessary and vital element.

Fire (화)

What would happen to life if there were no sun? Its value is self-explanatory. The same is true for our bodies. The energy of fire that flows throughout the human body gives each of us vitality. A low body temperature indicates that fire energy is weak, leading to all kinds of diseases: chills, indigestion, infertility, poor circulation, obesity, and cancer are just some of the ailments that stem from multiple factors—including too little fire energy. While indigestion may be related to the nerves, a body suffering from indigestion also isn't delivering sufficient heat to the stomach. Yoga practitioners in India call the practice of purifying the digestive system *agni sara*, meaning "fire energy."

Heat is necessary for digestion, and one can't be comfortable with an upset stomach. It's hard to move with vigor if your core is weak. That's why, in Korea, it was long customary to greet our elders by asking, "Is your inside comfortable? (속은 편하십니까?)" Just as a seed can't sprout when it's too cold or too hot, women who bare their bellies and make their lower bodies cold have a higher chance of infertility. The same applies to men who consume too much meat and alcohol and lead high-stress, unpredictable lifestyles. These conditions make it hard for egg and sperm to thrive.

We live in an age where many populations around the world now eat cold food taken directly from the fridge, so it's also important to pay attention to the temperature of the food being eaten. Eating food at the same temperature as the human body prevents shocking the body's cells and gives rise to the energy of fire, aiding the ability to absorb nutrients and digest food.

All the behaviors above make the body cold and thus aren't good for us. But there are things we can do to stoke our inner fires. Just as a seed sprouts in warmth, walking in the sunlight or engaging in other aerobic exercises can amplify the fire energy in our bodies and restore our vitality. This is the flow of life.

Wind (풍)

Wind holds the nature of movement and ventilation. It sustains matter and makes it move. Like breath, the wind circulates and blows life into the body. When we eat, wind energy propels food through our bodies, creating space for replenishment and releasing harmful matter. The wind element acts as nature's windpipe, connecting all plants, animals, and humans in the universe. It gives breath to our lungs and revives a dying spark through a bellow. Stronger winds, like those of a storm, can cause damage but also have the opposite effect of cleaning the deep ocean. What other force on earth could purify the depths of the ocean? Only tides carried by the wind can do this. The wind moves everything, sometimes with strength and at other times gently. It propels life.

The human body consists of elemental earth, water, fire, and wind and achieves harmony through the power of emptiness. Emptiness is the flower of harmony that enables these four elements to exist, thrive, and break down for regeneration. This is the ultimate energy of harmonious creativity that gives life to all things through the sun, the clouds, the wind, and the earth.

This emptiness can be understood broadly as the principle of universal life rather than a purely physiological phenomenon. Thus, emptiness is integral to the human spirit. When our spirits are low, our energy drops. But when the spirit is pure, our energy is unhindered.

Emptiness also facilitates one's awakening. When we look into our hearts, feel the flow of our minds and bodies, and pay attention to our senses, we realize that all sensations are merely a desire for experience. Emptiness is a foundational source of energy that makes us observe our unnecessary attachments. Through the power of emptiness, we can simply be ourselves and harmonize with others, allowing them to also be themselves.

A Meal of Oheng

The four elements—earth, water, fire, and wind—are the raw matter that make up the foundation of human life. All food is made of this matter. The relationship between the mind and body can be explained through *Oheng*,[5] which describes the cycle and relationships of five elements; wood, fire, earth, metal, and water. The interactions of these five elements demonstrate how all things in creation must cooperate and collide with one another. We must practice the wisdom of understanding things from the context of their relationships to one another. For example, the body relies on the mind, and the mind cannot exist without the body, so when just one is out of balance, it's hard to escape a life of suffering. Everything we eat consists of the four raw elements and nutrients, and a meal of *Oheng* is a strong connective thread that ties everything together.

Oheng Theory of wood, fire, earth, metal, and water is represented by the colors green, red, yellow, white, and black, respectively. In the body, they correspond to the liver, heart, stomach, lungs, and kidneys. They also symbolize the five tastes: sour, bitter, sweet, spicy, and salty. *Oheng* is also represented in the seasons of spring, summer, center, fall, and winter. But to understand this concept, you can't rely on formulaic logic. Instead, you must use the wisdom and insight of harmony and fluidity.

---

5 *Oheng* (오행): Five Element Theory, an ancient Chinese philosophy. Korean Zen Buddhism originated from India yet went through a heavy influence of ancient Chinese culture before reaching Korea. Thus, its belief has the combined view of ancient India's four elements (earth, water, fire, wind) and ancient China's five elements (wood, fire, earth, metal, water). While all things are thought to be made of four "raw" elements, their relationships including human body, mind, and food are explained according to the Five Element Theory.

Wood (목) represents the strength of a spring sprout bursting through the firm, late-winter earth. Spring greens are full of restorative energy and possess the power to awaken humans and animals. If winter is a time of rest and recharge, foods with wood energy arrive after winter and support winter's metal energy. Green foods contain beta-carotene that helps  release harmful germs from the body and accelerates the secretion of new hormones. The green sprouts of spring wake up the liver and brighten the eyes as we absorb their tartness. It is said that staring at the color green is naturally good for the eyes, so how much better must eating nature's greens be? For example, the eyes and the liver have a close relationship, like that of a parent and child. An unhealthy liver results in poor eyesight, which is why a disease like cirrhosis is often accompanied by jaundice.

Eating green food is good for not only the liver but also the lungs. As the five elements of *Oheng* are interconnected, wood acts as an agent that helps form blood cells by producing plenty of chlorophyll. Iron-rich greens like spinach, broccoli, and peppers can lower cholesterol due to their ability to restore cells. The color green contains the energy of wood and signifies the matter that creates all living things.

Fire (화) is a burst of passion and vitality—an extreme state of yang energy, which is the expansion of the wood energy of spring. On a blazingly hot summer day, we can instantly quench our thirst by taking a big bite from a red watermelon plucked from a field. It is expressed as a fiery, flashy red. Summertime is when our bodies receive heat and rise in temperature, making us sweat and seek cold things for replenishment. Just as we search for shade to escape the summer heat, our cells seek food that can lower our temperature.

Without a reprieve from the heat, no one can predict what kind of explosion may happen in our bodies. Surely, we would die of heatstroke. So naturally, we look for cold food to cool the intense heat. Before refrigeration, it was customary in Korea to place a bowl of cool barley rice under a home's eaves and eat it with water. Just as we consume warm food or bathe in warm water when our bodies become too cold, we seek cold food to prevent the heart from filling with gas.

The primary color of fire is red. Red foods function as antioxidants because they contain anthocyanin, which removes active oxygen radicals. They also prevent and improve cardiovascular diseases and aid with memory. Tomatoes have lycopene, one of the most effective antioxidants, which helps to prevent and treat kidney disease, prostate cancer, and lung cancer. Red foods with plenty of vitamins B and C are best consumed boiled rather than raw to bring out more lycopene. It can take the liver at least four or five hours to break down tomatoes, so they are best consumed before meals. Spiciness helps to release heat as well.

During the summer, the weather forecast includes a "discomfort index" because heat brings the element of fire to the body and excitement to the mind, making it helpful to anticipate discomfort in advance. The color red is also used to fight bad energy, which is why it is tradition to eat red bean porridge on the winter solstice and hang red chili peppers on the door to block evil spirits from entering a house after giving birth to a son.

Earth (토) is an elemental energy that is harmonious, firm, and steadfast. The nature of soil is consideration and mediation—the earth enables everything to grow and embraces all things with warmth. The ground acts as the central intermediary during the four seasons—spring, summer, fall, and winter—facilitating the seasonal transitions and allowing plants and seeds to mature internally with its generous energy. The earth element is silent yet firmly holds the center of all things. It's represented by the color yellow, which harmonizes with green and red. Earth element is associated with the stomach and spleen in the body's center. The stomach is aligned with the spinal cord, which influences the expression of many human genes. If food isn't properly digested by the stomach, the expression of certain genes may mutate and create mutated proteins, which can cause cancer. That's why cancer or kidney disease patients can often benefit from eating yellow foods. Improper digestion also blocks other organs, so it's essential to eat food that can aid digestion.

Yellow foods like sweet potatoes, pumpkins, carrots, and oranges make us feel good with their sweet tastes. They carry beta-carotene and ease our nerves. Carrots, particularly, clear our minds and aid the autonomous nervous system. Yellow foods also contain anti-inflammatory properties that are good for the body's cells and aid the immune system. They also have carotenoids, which are anticarcinogenic and combat allergies and bacteria.

Metal (금) element is the melancholy, white fruit of fall, characterized by a hard, cold, clean, and egalitarian nature. From early May to early August, roots underneath the ground gather nutrients. Then, fall ushers in the necessary time for their energies to build and ripen. The element of metal is associated with the lungs, two of the body's hardest-working organs. The lungs work tirelessly to lubricate the body by fighting foreign substances and relieving pressure in the blood. Fluid from the kidneys cycles to the lungs, so it's dangerous for the lungs to dry up and crackle. White root vegetables with a lot of mucin, like yams, lotus root, bellflower root (*doraji*), cabbage, radish, potatoes, burdock root (*ueong*), taro, and white beans, aid in the lubrication of the lungs. The isoflavones in white beans provide estrogen, which is effective in preventing osteoporosis and breast cancer, and also help lower cholesterol and ease symptoms of menopause. Foods like *doraji*, radish, and *deodeok* contain many anthoxanthins and flavonoids that circulate heat and support the lungs and bronchial tubes. They can also repress the side effects of active oxygens and improve immunity against harmful bacteria and viruses.

Eating at least one type of glutinous food a day can be beneficial. The sticky material in yams and taro hydrates and helps maintain moisture. Yams can be fried in the pan every morning or eaten as a liquid meal blended with some black soybean paste, yam powder, ginkgo powder, tuber fleeceflower root powder, and perilla powder at a ratio of 10:2:2:2:10.

The fall season produces many bitter plants, like persimmon, which can be pickled or turned into vinegar. Bitter root vegetables can be used to help mature the mind and body. We can enjoy the fall's abundance by fattening our minds with the pure, noble nature of these white foods, seeking to grow our own equanimity.

Water (수) element is represented by the color black, the winter season, and holds the nature of wisdom, adaptation, storage, rest, and emptiness. It is associated with the kidneys and bladder, as well as the taste profile of salt. The water element invites rest—a time of calm and reflection—just as the days are short and the nights long in winter. During water's winter season, it's advisable to adapt fluidly, like flowing water, and spend the long season in stillness rather than trying to be active. As water makes up most of the human body, we must consistently supply our bodies with moisture to prevent its cycles from growing stale and congested and preserve the wisdom of a mind and body held in a state of flow.

Early March is the time for gathering sap from trees like maple and birch. In Korean traditional herbal medicine, drinking water from a maple tree is prescribed for ailments like stomachache, a weak constitution, neuralgia, and arthritis. But just like a blood transfusion, this practice should be reserved only for those who absolutely need it. It's also essential to consider the wisdom of yin, yang, and the five phases, taking only the necessary amount of sap from the tree and looking after its health with love and care just as we look after our bodies.

Like sap from a tree, salt is medicine from the sea: the flower of the ocean and a repository for minerals. It is an essential ingredient that gives a pleasant taste to food and a vitality to life. Too much of it can become poison, but an appropriate amount of salt is necessary for a harmonious taste. Salt is associated with the kidneys and the bladder, where moisture gathers. This is why we restrict salt intake for people with nephritis.

Black foods good for the kidneys include black beans, black sesame seeds, kelp, and shiitake mushrooms. Deficient kidneys can lead to premature graying hair and baldness. The cells in our scalp are connected to our kidneys, so if they get inflamed, the hair follicles weaken, and we lose hair. I have a university friend who runs a book café in Chuncheon. They never take off their hat, even in the summer. One day, noticing my curiosity, my friend removed their hat to show me that they were suffering from hair loss caused by stress. I told them to wash their hair for three years with the water left over after boiling black soybeans. Upon visiting me several years later, their first words were, "*Seunim*, I no longer have to wear a hat!" I was surprised to see their lush black hair. They had listened to my words and used the black soybean water every time they washed their hair. I was grateful that they had endured the task with such patience and clasped my hands to give thanks for the power of the beans.

Black foods can clear the blood and improve kidney disease because they contain anthocyanin, which prevents the arteries from clotting. They also contain antioxidants, which sterilize inflammatory agents, and rhodopsin, which relieves eye fatigue.

Black sesame has similar benefits to black beans, particularly for the voice. So, if you talk a lot, it's good to eat it regularly. It also carries plenty of plant fat, so after eating it for three months, you can see your skin improve. Good skin signifies there's no trouble in the digestive tract and indicates that the peaceful nature of the color black is alive and well within the body system. I strongly recommend lifelong consumption of black beans, perilla seed powder, and tuber fleeceflower root powder, which will make your body as light and natural as Mother Nature herself, even as you grow old.

Even in the winter, beneath the frozen surface of nature's bodies of water, the energy of creation continues to breathe, storing the energy of yang to prepare for the arrival of spring. Water carries a strong yin energy but absorbs and stores the dynamic yang energy, releasing it slowly to assist the growth of greens once spring comes around.

The five elemental phases are in a state of constant flow. All matter constantly changes due to a profound, never-ending cycle of cause and effect. The four elements of earth, water, fire, and wind form the foundation of all things. The cycle of the five phases of wood, fire, earth, metal, and water carries us in their cosmic harmony. They are deeply embedded in our food culture, giving us a beautiful, balanced diet.

The Enzyme Effect

If our bodies can't digest food properly and suffer from poor metabolism, even a balanced meal prepared according to the principles of the four elements and *Oheng* can lead to a buildup of waste. Food may be medicine, but if the body can't break it down or absorb it properly, it simply passes through the system without providing nutrients. Foods that enter the body can't interact without the help of enzymes. Enzymes support the production of red blood cells and bone and interact with hormones and nerves to aid the activity of each organ. They're responsible for the foundational energy needed to maintain life. However, since the body doesn't create an endless supply of enzymes, it's necessary to maintain the balance of enzymes by blocking harmful factors. Things that upset the body's enzyme balance include the variety of additives in our food, alcohol, nicotine, and anything containing excessive salt and sugar. Let's compare the body to a building: protein is the cement that builds the foundation of bone, vitamins create a space where all systems work in harmony, minerals act as the steel support beams, and enzymes are the workers who keep the building's functions running well.

Now, let's observe the six interactions of enzymes: First, they aid digestion and nutrient absorption. Food mixes with saliva and passes through the throat to reach the stomach. Throughout this process, it encounters many enzymes, like ptyalin. These enzymes deliver nutrients through the bloodstream, even reaching the cells inside our peripheral nerves. Second, enzymes help food break down and enable waste to leave the body through sweat and urine. Third, they help sterilize and act as an antibiotic, carrying white blood cells to infectious areas, increasing the body's ability to heal and recover damaged cells and quickening the process of clearing infections. Fourth, enzymes strengthen the liver, break down toxins, and carry the potent sterilizing power of antibiotics against pyogenic bacteria. Fifth, they clean and detoxify toxins and waste in the blood, breaking them down and releasing them from the body. They manage cholesterol to improve circulation and make blood healthy and alkaline. Sixth, they activate cellular metabolic function, quickly replacing old cells with new ones.

A table of wisdom can be set with food made from a happy, sincere heart and in accordance with the nature of life; the pure and soft virtues of universal laws; the energies of earth, water, fire, and wind; and the harmonious colors of green, red, yellow, white, and black. If our meals consist of this kind of food, it will brighten our bodies, not to mention our hearts and minds.

Tasty Spicy Noodles
(Byeolmi Bibim Guksu)

When feeling depressed, the spiciness of *gochujang* can help you feel better. But overconsumption of spicy food can lead to impatience, so it's important to eat it in moderation. *Somyeon* (thin wheat flour noodles) are sometimes colored red with prickly pears (cactus fruit) or beets. You can also use regular *somyeon* for this recipe.

Ingredients

1 ounce dandelion leaves

7 ounces *somyeon* noodles

1 ounce *dolnamul* or *dotnamul* (*Sedum sarmentosum*) or other greens

Spicy sauce:

3 tablespoons *gochujang*

1 teaspoon *gochugaru* (Korean chili pepper)

1 tablespoon sesame oil

1 tablespoon sesame seeds

1 tablespoon *jocheong* (rice syrup)

2 tablespoons water

1 tablespoon white vinegar

Directions

1. The bitter taste of dandelion greens is great to invigorate taste buds. Prepare these greens by trimming them and washing in cold water. Drain well.

2.   In a small pot, mix together the spicy sauce ingredients, except the vinegar. Boil over medium heat for 3 minutes. Once the sauce is cooled, mix in the vinegar. You can also use this sauce to season other vegetables such as *minari* (Korean watercress) and mushrooms.

3.   Bring a pot of water to a boil and cook the noodles. Add about ½ cup of cold water to the boiling water if it reaches a rapid boil. This prevents the water from boiling over. Once cooked, rinse the noodles in cold water and drain.

4.   Put the noodles in a bowl, top with the greens, then serve with the sauce on the side. You can also mix the noodles with the sauce before serving.

Acorn Porridge
(Dotori Juk)

Acorns give off a color that is similar to shiitake mushrooms. Tannins in acorns can help improve mood when you feel depressed.

Ingredients

1 cup *dotori garu* (acorn starch powder)

3 cups water, plus more for soaking

1 teaspoon sesame oil

½ teaspoon salt

Garnish:

Small piece roasted *gim* (dried seaweed sheet)

½ tablespoon sesame seeds

Directions

1. Soak the acorn powder in cold water. Once the acorn sediment settles in the bottom of the bowl, carefully pour the water out.

2. Combine the acorn sediment with 3 cups of water in a saucepan, then bring to a boil over medium heat, stirring constantly with a wooden spoon.

3. When it comes to a boil, reduce the heat to low and simmer for 20 minutes. Mix in the sesame oil and salt to season at the end.

4. Cut the seaweed sheet into short, thin strips.

5. Serve the porridge warm in a bowl, topped with the seaweed pieces and sesame seeds.

Omija (Five-Flavor Berries) Jelly
(Omija Yanggaeng)

Omija (five-flavor berries or schisandra berries) have a cooling nature. Thus, *omija* jelly is a refreshing summer snack to cool down with during scorching days. It's easy to carry and great for eating while on the go.

Ingredients

¼ to ½ cup dried *omija* berries

2 cups cold water

1.5 ounces agar strips (or 2 teaspoons agar powder)

¼ cup *jocheong* (rice syrup)

4 ounces sweetened white bean paste

Directions

1. Prepare the *omija* liquid ahead. Rinse and drain the *omija* berries and soak them in 2 cups of cold water overnight.
2. Soak the agar in lukewarm water for a minimum of 2 hours.
3. Strain the 2 cups of *omija* liquid into a pot. Stir in the rice syrup and white bean paste. You can run the bean paste through a strainer if it doesn't mix well.
4. Bring the mixture to a boil, stirring with a wooden spoon.
5. Add the agar and continue cooking over medium heat, stirring, until the agar melts.
6. Remove the mixture from the heat and let it cool.

7. Pour the mixture into a mold. Keep it in the refrigerator for a few hours, then cut the jelly into slices. For kids or for gifting to someone, you may use fun-shaped silicone molds.

part three

A
Harmonious
Table

The number of vegetarian restaurants and grocery stores is growing as more people become aware that a vegetarian diet is good for their health and the environment. Following this trend, there's also increased research on how to cook vegetables in more dynamic and enjoyable ways and the availability of new and unique hybrid varieties of produce. For example, much produce is now grown inside greenhouses to control the temperature in a rapidly changing climate. But it's still a shame the farming industry uses so many pesticides and machines instead of weeding by hand. I pray for the day we can harvest all crops organically.

Many people who have tried a vegetarian diet for various reasons say they feel better inside and clearer-headed. Eating seasonally is the best way to enjoy the utmost benefit from a vegetarian diet. For example, eating cucumbers—a summer vegetable—in the winter can cause a cold. But eating colorful food according to the harmony of the seasons is one way to care for the body.

Temple food is nutritious and harmonious, made from simple ingredients and just a few sauces and seasonings. Using too much seasoning can make all greens taste similar, even though each is unique. If *minari*,[1] mugwort, and *naengi* pancakes all taste the same, there wasn't a proper balance of oil and fire in the cooking process.

Temple cuisine preserves and presents each ingredient's natural scent and flavor without artificial seasonings and sweeteners. Instead, we use natural seasonings like mushroom powder, kelp powder, perilla seed powder, sesame, and bean powder. Even with these, we use only a little to balance

---

1 *Minari* (미나리): water celery/water dropwort or Korean watercress, a fragrant green plant used extensively in Korean and other East Asian cooking

taste or nutrients. Everything is kept very simple. For this reason, temple kitchens don't smell of food for too long. Only a freshness remains, like the smile of a wildflower or a friendly hug between neighbors.

Two quintessential Korean foods, *doenjang* and *kimchi*, are fermented. In the temple, we've begun experimenting with various ways to store them: for example, in the shade and in the sun, half yin and half yang. We make sure to use the appropriate timing and method of fermentation to bring out the trait of each ingredient. Korea's fermented foods are famous the world over for allowing microorganisms to secrete all kinds of enzymes that help the body absorb food. *Kimchi* is especially popular in Japan, the United States, and Europe, leading many enthusiastic foreign chefs to learn how to make cabbage *kimchi*, as well as with other native Korean ingredients.

Pickles and vinegar are also fermented, shelf-stable foods. They're popular health foods because they help the body absorb nutrients; release waste; and lower cholesterol, which can cause the arteries to thicken and lead to various diseases.

In the old days, households would store food ahead of winter. In Korea, these foods include fermented tofu, preserved persimmons, and steamed or dried sweet potatoes. We invented a variety of preserved foods like persimmon vinegar and pickled persimmons, salting and fermenting the fruit appropriately to bring out its flavor and facilitate absorption. These foods have been passed down from generation to generation as they are easy to store, minimize the destruction of nutrients, and solve the risk of nutrient imbalance due to a lack of vegetables. Temples have played an essential role in preserving this tradition.

If we know our ingredients, they can become medicine of their own—easy to digest if cooked according to their nature. When the energy and blood in the body circulate smoothly, it naturally produces a medicinal effect. Food and medicine harmonize to deliver us vibrant energy. Seasonal ingredients aid in recovering health just as medicinal herbs do.

Fermented food is the crown jewel of natural food. Fermentation occurs as microorganisms secrete various enzymes in an undisturbed, natural environment. The final product aids digestion and gets rid of chemical toxins. Fermented foods include *kimchi*, *doenjang*, soy sauce, fermented soybeans, *gochujang*, vinegar, and a rice beverage called *sikhye*.[2] Not only do fermented foods add depth of flavor, but they also lower cholesterol, act as anticarcinogens, and prevent various diseases.

The way fermented food is prepared is a practice in and of itself. We must use seasonal ingredients and follow the step-by-step process of fermentation. Making *doenjang* is one example—a complicated process that requires fresh, organic beans, sea salt, and fresh water. First, soybeans are threshed from the field in the autumn. Then, they're made into *meju* (fermented soybean blocks). Once the blocks are complete, they're dried through the winter and are made into *doenjang* in the first month of the lunar year.

Wash and dry the *meju* before putting them in an empty pot. Then, add clean water at about 18% salinity, charcoal, dried chili pepper, and dried kelp. Close the lid and tie a straw string around it. Then, wait for it to ferment. After sixty days, remove the fermented bean blocks from the pot and rub them gently before breaking them down. The crumbled blocks can

---

2 *Sikhye* (식혜): a sweetened Korean beverage made with rice and malt

be returned to the pot for storage. Place a hemp cloth over the opening and sprinkle it with salt to ward off insects. Then, seal the pot tightly by wrapping it in a sheet of paper like *hanji* or a cloth like *bojagi*. You can eat the *doenjang* after one year, but the longer it ferments, the richer it tastes. You can also use the water left over from the pot to make a rich and delicious homemade soy sauce by fermenting it separately.

When the Australian chef Nick Flynn visited Balwoo Gongyang, he tasted *gochujang*, *doenjang*, and *ganjang* in rapid succession. Afterward, he exclaimed that it was an incredibly complex and elaborate taste. The experience probably provided him with an entirely new paradigm for making sauce.

Temple Ingredients

All plants foraged from the mountains and fields carry distinct characteristics in their roots, stems, leaves, flowers, and fruits. Not all roots contain the same nutrients; some parts are naturally warm, while others are cool. Still others are tasteless or colorless. Each part of a plant has a different property. The soil, temperature, climate, and environment for cultivation all affect the various nutrients delivered to us through leafy greens, mountain herbs, and root and vining vegetables.

Cabbage is a white plant that belongs to the category of leafy greens. White food is related to the element of metal and benefits the lungs and colon. Cabbage leaves aid in the digestion of grains through photosynthesis. They carry a sweet taste and possess the nature of the earth element. The whole cabbage can be cooked. It's good for the stomach and is especially beneficial for those who have warmer bodies. Steaming it is better than eating it raw in terms of nutrients and absorption.

Most mountain herbs are green. They are detoxifiers that are good for the liver. The phytochemicals function as antioxidants, preventing aging. However, mountain herbs are potent and must be used in accordance with their nature.

Most white root vegetables grow their roots deep within the earth to maintain their characteristics. They're filled with nutrients that are good for the bones, lungs, and intestines. Lotus root grows in wet soil and contains the nature of metal. Its holed appearance resembles a muscle attached to bone. The Korean medical text, *Dongui Bogam*, states that drinking the juice from lotus root and sleeping in a warm room helps relieve muscle pain. This is because the lotus root helps to grow the cells in bones, joints, and ligaments. Considering how healthy lungs produce bone cells, you could also say lotus root helps the lungs. White root vegetables provide the necessary moisture and humidity required for healthy lungs.

Vegetables like squash grow in one lump. These are called vining vegetables. They carry the element of earth, taste sweet, and help the stomach, pancreas, and gallbladder. Each vegetable has a different taste and scent, and in temple cuisine, we use a vegetable's taste more so than its scent to help the body.

This is why vegetables with distinct characteristics in each part of their structures are best cooked according to their nature.

Mushrooms and Tofu

Fall is the season of mushrooms, though today, we can get them whenever we want at the supermarket. But even twenty years ago, it was difficult to find mushrooms out of season. While it's important to eat seasonally, at times, it's also wise to receive proper nutrients with a flexible approach to ingredients.

When it comes to mushrooms, we say the first is the hedgehog, the second is shiitake, and the third is matsutake/pine. The shingled hedgehog mushroom can be gathered in September in areas with many oaks or along a mountain ridge if there's quality soil. Since they're rare mushrooms that can't be cultivated, we treat them carefully. You can store them with salt or dry them in the shade to preserve their scent, which is so strong it can linger for an entire day if you make shingled hedgehog mushroom tea or eat them raw.

In October, the matsutake mushrooms begin to raise their heads above the pine fields and are ready to be gathered. These mushrooms are usually served roasted and dipped in salt and sesame sauce, but you can also steam them in pumpkin leaves to enjoy their pure taste. I typically make mushroom summer squash dumplings that are soft in taste and scent. To make the dumplings, thinly slice the mushrooms and squash, add some sesame oil and bamboo salt, then mash it together. Spoon the mixture into dumpling wrappers and steam them for about ten minutes. When they're ready, the scent of the mushrooms will fill up the entire kitchen.

Chanterelles can be gathered around the same time of year as pine and morel mushrooms. They're small and difficult to find, but since they always grow in the same spots, you only need to know their location to gather them easily. In Korea, these mushrooms are called "nightingale mushrooms" because they resemble the shape of a nightingale singing with its head raised. They're a mixture of yellow and orange and spread out like a big, beautiful carpet in a healthy growth environment. You can bring out their best scent by stir-frying them with perilla oil and summer squash. Chanterelles are often used as an additional ingredient in mushroom-based dishes.

Coral mushrooms are becoming harder to gather as they aren't cultivated as frequently as they once were, although some can still be found near the Mungyeong and Sangju areas of Korea. Edible coral mushrooms are tasty and popular in China and Japan. They must be prepared by being steamed and simmered, then stir-fried. Their scent is quite unique.

Chestnut mushrooms and lion's mane are also edible, best served blanched and dipped in *gochujang*. A dish of sweet and sour mushrooms is a slightly more complex way to cook these ingredients—essentially an assortment of vegetables and shiitake mushrooms deep-fried in starch. It's a popular item that's always on the menu at any temple event and a long-running staple at vegetarian restaurants. The dish I usually make is mushroom *chilbochae*, which consists of seven types of mushrooms and seven different vegetables. The mushrooms aren't deep-fried but stir-fried. Its harmonious scent and flavor make it a favorite among many.

Mushrooms can be steamed and spiced with red chili powder, served to the whole family in a hot pot, or eaten as *pyeonyuk* (cold cuts) along with various nuts. Mushroom *pyeonyuk* is made by putting agar in the mushrooms as a filler and then firming them up in a mold for their shape. *Pyeonyuk*'s texture becomes just like meat.

Oyster, enoki, and button mushrooms can be roasted, steamed, or made into pancakes. Every holiday at the temple, we make three-colored roasted mushroom skewers with shiitake mushrooms, carrots, and *minari*. It's very popular among the monks.

Mushrooms may be the first ingredient to have awakened to the Buddhist concept of selflessness and emptiness. They don't have their own bodies but grow like parasites on a host, surviving by spreading spores—no different from how humans depend on our parents to progenate—first living as one complete spore before enabling us to grow, live our lives, and die.

**

Tofu is another quintessential temple food. This fermented staple came to Korea by way of a monk who studied in China during the Tang Dynasty. The earliest mention of tofu is in the text written by the scholar Yi Saek[3] (1328-1396): "Even vegetable porridge tastes bland after a while, but tofu has brought in a new flavor to restore health to this old body." Scholar Gwon Geun[4] (1352-1400) describes the process of making tofu: "The yellow ripe beans are boiled in a fiery cauldron, turning the water snowy white, which is then carefully removed. The cooks lift the heavy, well-oiled cauldron lid to pull out what looks like a jade block, slicing it and piling it high on the dinner table." Making tofu has always been effortful. In temples located in dense woods, for example, self-sustained mills were built to make rice cake and tofu, providing much-needed protein, though operating the mills required strenuous effort.

Records on tofu show that during the Joseon Dynasty, the Joseon Kingdom endeavored to minimize Buddhism in favor of Confucianism. As a part of these efforts, temples were built around the royal gravesite. Records also show that tofu, traditionally made in these Buddhist temples, was then made for Confucian rituals. Today, tofu remains a symbol of Buddhist temple food.

---

3 Yi Saek (이색): Also known by his pen name Mogeun (목은), Yi Saek was a Neo-Confucian scholar and poet whose academy produced pupils that later went on to form the Joseon Dynasty.
4 Gwon Geun (권근): A disciple of Yi Saek, Gwon Geun was a Neo-Confucian scholar who had considerable influence on the formation of the Joseon Dynasty.

Lecithin, which is found inside beans, makes up 30% of our brain's dry weight and supplies it with lipids. It also makes up the cell membrane in our body and surrounds the trapped fat in the bloodstream, helping it move. This lecithin is also a source of acetylcholine, which delivers information to the brain and prevents cellular aging. Eating bean dishes in the winter is optimal because beans are full of fats and proteins—a good energy source. They also keep heat from escaping the body. Beans are beneficial for the brain and provide quality nutrients. Our ancestors would grow bean sprouts in their houses to compensate for the lack of vitamins during wintertime. Today, bean sprouts are easy to buy, but years ago, it was hard to get them unless you grew them yourself.

Tofu is also made of beans—grinding and boiling soaked beans, then adding salt water before clotting them. Tofu has a 95% digestion rate. By contrast, roasting raw beans only gives you a 60% digestion rate. Fermented foods like *doenjang* give you 85%, and fermented tofu gives you 100%.

The tofu hot pot is one of the best dishes to eat in winter. To make it, neatly arrange mushrooms, radishes, shiitake, other various vegetables, and kelp in a pot. Boil them in vegetable stock and season with *doenjang*, *gochujang*, and red chili powder. For *doenjang jjigae*, boil the tofu and radish before adding *doenjang*, sliced red pepper, and red chili powder. For fermented tofu soup, boil sliced radish, *kimchi*, and tofu in vegetable stock. Steamed tofu is made with tofu, radish, and dried shiitake mushrooms. Use red chili powder, soy sauce, perilla oil, and plenty of water to boil over a lengthy period. The sweetness of the radish, the flavor of the tofu, and the spicy seasoning blend well to make you forget the cold. To make preserved tofu, fry it until it's yellow and pour boiled water over it. Tofu is also used for dumplings on Seollal, the Korean New Year. The water must be squeezed out of the tofu before frying it in a pan with salt and sesame oil. This makes it easier for the dumpling fillings to mix together.

The old texts mention fermented tofu, which was made by wrapping it in cloth and storing it inside a *doenjang* pot until it was taken out to be consumed once it started gaining water. During the first month of the year, homemade *kimchi* was consumed with tofu. Thus, tofu has existed since the old days as a benevolent presence that alleviated hunger.

Goji

Red goji berries are medicinal plants that are easy to find in Korean markets. They protect the liver and kidneys, supplant stamina, and carry no poison or adverse side effects. The only downside to goji berries is that they're so healthful even insects love them. Since goji protects the kidneys, it's also good for the eyes. It's effective for treating high blood pressure and neuralgia, strengthening the back, and preventing cancer. Goji can even alleviate constipation and gastric ulcers. It acts like a cure-all medicine.

Goji is usually consumed as a tea, but you can also make rice cakes, porridge, and scones. It's better to eat processed berries rather than raw ones because their sweetness is so intense that the use of pesticides to prevent bugs is inevitable. To clean the berries, dip them nine times in alcohol (*soju* is a great option) and dry them. This process will make them flavorful and give them a nice sheen before cooking them into a healthy and tasty dish or preparing them as a delicious tea.

Eggplant

Eggplant consists of 93% water and is rich in protein, carbohydrates, calcium, vitamins, and minerals. It strengthens the function of the intestines, helping with constipation and other bowel conditions. Its polyphenols suppress carcinogens. Due to its high dose of vitamins, it's also good for alleviating fatigue. Given eggplant's cold nature, eating it consistently can help with inflammation and fever. You can prepare eggplant in a variety of ways, including as a summer salad, cold soup, and pancakes. Fried eggplant salad with vegetables and yuzu dressing is a beautiful dish, as is stuffed eggplant with mushrooms. These are all healthy options.

We harvested so many eggplants one year that I created a pasta dish to use them all. To make eggplant pasta, peel the skin, steam it, and blend it in a mixer with half a cup of milk. Boil the mixture in a pot and add mozzarella. Once the cheese becomes melted and fragrant, put in the pasta. Simmer until the sauce thickens, and you'll get an aromatic, delicious dish.

Mustard Greens

Fall is a season of preparation for the winter. It's also when Koreans make *kimchi*. Incorporating mustard greens into the cabbage prevents the *kimchi* from getting mushy. When ripened, these greens generate estrogen, fortify iron, and grow even richer in flavor and nutrients. Once aged, they are rich in lactic acid bacteria, which aids digestion and intestinal circulation. The bacteria created in this process are plant-based, not animal-based like those found in yogurt, and therefore can be entirely absorbed by the body, accomplishing their role without dying.

Sweet Potatoes

A variety of sweet potatoes are available throughout Korea. They're popular as a weight loss aid and used as pizza toppings in Korea. Sweet potato is excellent at maintaining moisture, meaning it's good for the skin. (It is said that "to become beautiful, one must eat sweet potatoes.") But eat too much, and you might experience indigestion. That's why Korea's ancestors passed down the wisdom of eating *kimchi* alongside sweet potatoes. Purple and pumpkin sweet potatoes have twenty times as many antioxidants as regular sweet potatoes.

Fried sweet potato *japchae* rolls make a great snack. The conventional fried *japchae* noodles wrapped in seaweed are often too oily, so I developed a new recipe to replace them. First, mash the sweet potatoes and season with salt and sesame oil. Spread them over the dried seaweed, add *japchae* noodles, and then roll it up. Batter lightly before frying, then drain the oil. This is a healthy, tasty snack that even children can enjoy.

Buckwheat

Buckwheat flowers contain rutin and amino acids. When grinding buckwheat, it's best to peel off the external skin only. Buckwheat is black food, and its rutin helps prevent artery hardening, high blood pressure, glaucoma, diabetes, and cancer. It's also effective against constipation, diarrhea, hiccups, gum disease, and bad breath. Buckwheat is a cold food and can be made into a powder to be consumed with honey or cooked as noodles, jelly, and pancakes. For people with cooler bodies, it's good to eat buckwheat with radish to benefit digestion and the eradication of toxins.

Deodeok (Codonopsis Root)

Walking in the mountains, you can smell the bitter scent of *deodeok* tempting your tastebuds and nostrils. The primary component of *deodeok* is saponin—the same as ginseng. For this reason, it has been used as food and medicine for a long time. Wild mountain *deodeok* has a strong scent and potent medicinal properties. The pooled water inside old *deodeok* was once considered the medicine of eternal youth.

Deodeok is used to lower blood pressure, promote breast milk production, make blood, and treat fatigue. It can also be used as a digestive or tonic. You can enjoy the full scent of *deodeok* by eating it raw as a salad. To cook it, grill it slightly in a pan with a bit of sesame oil, *gochujang*, and *jocheong* (rice syrup). Pickled *deodeok* harvested in the fall has an even deeper scent and bolder taste.

Doraji (Bellflower Root)

The root of a bellflower carries magical properties, just like its beautiful white and purple flowers that resemble stars. *Doraji* is as effective as ginseng, especially for treating a cold or bronchitis. It's used to prevent aging, treat a hangover, help with nephritis, and is an effective diuretic. The *Dongui Bogam* lists 278 uses of *doraji*, namely its ability to supply blood and warm the body, boosting circulation. This precious plant is a root vegetable that alleviates cough and phlegm and soothes a sore throat. To prepare *doraji*, boil the root with honey and sip it slowly while warm.

Bellflower root is so strong that its essential oil—the cause of its extremely pungent taste—can even be used to remove mold. Placing the root in water neutralizes the pungency. Roots gathered in the spring can be sliced and stir-fried with sesame oil and soy sauce to bring out their full flavor. When you're sick with a cold, you can boil it down as a tonic or tea. Otherwise, eating it consistently as *banchan* will fill your body with vigor.

Green Plum

The plum blossoms that bloom in spring boast a graceful figure and a delightful scent that can be brought out in green tea or herb tea. When the seed hiding inside the flower sprouts, it becomes a plum, which usually gets pickled or made into syrup. Adding rice syrup and soy sauce to pickled plum and then chopping it makes for a handy ingredient whenever you need something sweet, like in preparing *bibimbap*. The citric acid in plums helps overcome the heat and is effective for sterilization, preventing food poisoning, and treating gastrointestinal troubles. People with excess stomach acid can eat a spoonful of plum syrup before a meal. Plums are an alkaline food good for indigestion, diarrhea, and fatigue.

Dandelion

If you sprinkle dandelion seeds in the backyard or garden, you can see the flowers raise their heads the following year. There are hundreds of distinct types of dandelions around the world, but the white variety that grows in Korea has the best medicinal properties. The properties of a dandelion include carotenoids, taraxacin, terpenoids, triterpenes, choline, tannins, sterol, various minerals, sodium, calcium, magnesium, iron, zinc, beta-carotene, and vitamins. If you pluck the roots, you'll find white sap, which is a natural antibiotic. Rubbing dandelion sap on an injury produces an anti-inflammatory effect. Raw dandelion leaves can be extracted and consumed every morning and night to treat gastrointestinal problems. According to the *Korean Encyclopedia of Medicinal Herbs*, dandelion helps with constipation, acute mastitis, and acute urethritis. Holding dandelion-steeped water in your mouth helps cure a sore throat. It's also used for jaundice and can help remedy a cloudy cornea. For burns, you can put the pulverized flower on the injured area. It is also an effective wart remover. Dandelions can be consumed as an extract or eaten raw by incorporating them in a salad or vegetable wrap, or drying the roots and making them into a powder.

Lettuce

Based on the ancient Egyptian mural depicting a person eating lettuce, the produce dates back to around 4,500 BCE; it is an ancient vegetable that is extremely easy to cultivate. For an abundance of lettuce, one only needs to plant five seedlings and give them plenty of water. They'll soon grow into lettuces ready to pluck. Our ancestors called it the "vegetable of a thousand pieces of gold."

Once you know the benefits of lettuce, you won't take it for granted just because it's so common. Lettuce is consumed the world over for its abundance of iron, which clears the blood and improves circulation. It's a cold food that eases anger, clears the head, eliminates insomnia, and boosts energy. It's rich in cellulose and vitamins, making it an effective prevention against arteriosclerosis and high blood pressure. Lettuce is beneficial if you have blood in your urine or are trying to increase breast milk production. The white extract on the end of the lettuce acts as a pacifier and contains lactoferrin and lactucin, which whitens the teeth and clears the blood. Lettuce is especially healthful for women due to its abundance of vitamins A and B, iron, calcium, and essential amino acids like lysine. Iron and amino acids help prevent anemia, while calcium and vitamin A help prevent postmenopausal osteoporosis. Lettuce also acts as a detoxifying agent and a diuretic, making it suitable for curing hangovers, insomnia, fatigue, and constipation, as well as boosting skin health.

Wrapping lightly grilled tofu in lettuce can almost mirror the sensation of eating meat. Slices of lightly seasoned and roasted soy protein also go well in lettuce wraps. Tofu made with fresh seawater can be eaten as-is, but tofu processed with seasoned water as most store-bought types must be blanched or soaked in hot water first before eating.

Chonggakmu (Ponytail Radish)

Chonggakmu, or ponytail radish, is named after the shape of a young man's hair.[5] To choose the best radish, select those with lighter leaves and stems, fewer small roots, and a soft sheen. The top of the radish should be green in color and moderate in thickness and length. Instead of peeling, wash the vegetables thoroughly to preserve the vitamin C in the skin. Ponytail radish alleviates a cough due to its moisture content and vitamin C. It's effective at preventing a cold when consumed in a boiled-down

---

5 *Chonggak* (총각): unmarried male. The young radish was named so because unmarried men used to wear their hair braided and tied into a long ponytail during Joseon era. Once married, his hair was made into a topknot called *sangtu* (상투).

state and helps to boost circulation and speed up recovery even after a cold. It also has anti-inflammatory properties that help with headaches and bleeding gums. You can put in various soups with *doenjang* or dry it for consumption in winter. Radish contains ten times as much vitamin C as an apple and has plenty of calcium and minerals that are good for preventing osteoporosis.

Korean Zucchini (Summer Squash)

Summer squash consists of 88% water, though this varies depending on the species. It contains a small amount of fructose, maltose, and dextrins. Compared to other types of squash, it has less dietary fiber, making it more easily digestible. This also makes it suitable for someone with a weak stomach or patients in recovery. The glucose in ripe summer squash contains a lot of starch and natural sugar, so it's sweet without adding extra seasoning. It also has a lot of water that can help supply moisture in the summer when we sweat. Compared to many vegetables, summer squash has more calories and sugar, vitamins E, C, B1, and niacin (B3). Summer squash also contains manganese and zinc. Zinc is a necessary component for growth, reproduction, and immunity. It also interacts with growth hormones. Dried summer squash carries a lot of fat-soluble vitamins like vitamins A and E, which can be absorbed easily when stir-fried in oil. The same goes for beta-carotene. To prepare the squash, wash it thoroughly, slice it, and dry it in the sun and wind. This increases the potassium content tenfold.

Peas

Soft, sweet peas contain carotene, vitamin C, choline, chlorophyll, and amino acids. They contain more vitamin A and plant fiber than other beans and six times as much glutamic acid as tomatoes. Peas help prevent osteoporosis, high blood pressure, and cancer, as well as lower cholesterol, suppress diabetes, and stimulate the brain. They help to prevent aging and weight gain and are healthy enough to eat with every meal. When making a steamed dish, you can mix in mashed peas. To add a light green coloring to noodles or dumplings, grind peas onto the dish. For something special, use ground peas to make fried cutlets similar to *tonkatsu* (fried pork or chicken cutlet).

Gajuk Shoots (Tree of Heaven Shoots)

Gajuk trees are named as fake (*ga*) bamboo (*juk*) trees. The dried and fried shoots called *gajukjaban* are a well-known dish in Korea. The young leaves are plucked in April and May, often blanched and eaten as wraps. You can also dry them and add *gochujang* for roasting later. These shoots can also be turned into fried snacks (*gajukjaban*). No matter how you prepare and eat them, their scent is very unique. In herbal medicine, the skins of the tree of heaven roots are gathered in the spring and fall to be used for alleviating dysentery, leukorrhea, diarrhea, hemorrhoids, and stomach ulcers. However, eating too much tree of heaven can cause severe diarrhea, headaches, and absent-mindedness. In the old days, people made *kimchi* with the greens, and eating the leaves as a salad or pickle was common, too. Rice cake made with the leaves and *gochujang* is a very special treat indeed.

Shiitake Mushroom

Shiitake mushrooms are harvested in the spring, summer, and fall. They help increase energy and promote a feeling of fullness. Their high-quality fiber helps prevent cholesterol absorption, and their vitamin D and calcium content encourages bone growth, making shiitakes especially beneficial for children with weak bones. Their vitamin E, F, and lecithin content helps prevent cholesterol from remaining in the blood. Their eritadenine can lower blood pressure, and the glucose content makes it an anti-tumorous plant. KS-2 helps prevent common diseases like the cold and activates the body's antivirals to fight influenza. Drinking shiitake mushroom tea is good for osteoporosis as well as skincare.

Pine Mushroom/Matsutake Mushroom

The *Dongui Bogam* describes pine mushrooms thus: "Pine mushrooms taste as they smell and carry the energy of pine trees because they grow beneath old pines in the mountains. This makes them the best mushrooms that grow from trees." Pine mushrooms are also called the "prince of mushrooms." In the *Veritable Records of the Joseon Dynasty*,[6] there's a record of these mushrooms being sent to the Ming Dynasty during the reign of King Sejong, which serves as proof of their excellence. Hearty pine mushrooms will have the film of their white fur intact, stout stems, and a clear white color. They're rich in proteins, vitamin B2, and vitamin D. The guanylic acid in these fungi produces its scent and taste. Pine mushrooms are an excellent dietary option since they're low in calories and help with heart disease by lowering cholesterol and blood pressure. They're also good

---

6 The *Veritable Records of the Joseon Dynasty* is a collection of annals of the Joseon Dynasty from 1392 to 1865. It was compiled by historians who kept extensive records on the reign of each monarch. It's thought to be the longest continuous record of a single dynasty.

to eat if suffering from a backache or knee ache. Pine mushrooms help the function of the stomach and intestines, circulate energy throughout the body, boost strength, and help reduce numbness in the hands and feet. The polysaccharides can even function as anticarcinogens.

When preparing, wash these mushrooms quickly to preserve their scent, tear them, and eat them raw, dipped in a mixture of ground sesame and salt. You can also roast or stir-fry pine mushrooms and mix them with other ingredients into rice, porridge, or pancakes.

Temple Flavors

People who taste temple food for the first time are usually astonished by nature's fresh aromas and tastes. They tilt their heads in wonder, saying they're unable to stop eating despite the austerity of the food. Though it's not oily or sweet, temple food stimulates the taste buds with a fresh and fragrant flavor. It captivates people by presenting them with a taste of nature simply enhanced through the use of vegetable stock and spices.

Dashima (Dried Kelp)

Kelp is the primary ingredient responsible for making temple food tasty. You can make a simple kelp stock by mixing an equal amount of kelp powder and shiitake powder, or dried kelp and dried shiitake, in a pot of water and boiling for ten minutes. Simmering kelp for too long can produce a bitter taste, making it sticky and dense. Adding well-prepared kelp stock to a dish makes it sweeter and softer. Along with seaweed, kelp is known as a repository of minerals, containing vitamin E, calcium, ash, and alginic acid—which produces the kelp's stickiness and acts as a sponge that absorbs metal, carcinogens, and pesticides, eliminating them from the body. It also absorbs bile acid inside the intestine to prevent it from being absorbed internally and helps with constipation and blood pressure. Dried kelp aids in minimizing thyroid diseases and helps prevent colorectal cancer by stimulating the organ. Its vitamin C and E content promotes glowing skin. It can also prevent osteoporosis because it's rich in bone-enhancing calcium, magnesium, and vitamin K2. Kelp stock can be added to all types of soup and stew dishes like *kimchi jjigae*, mushroom hot pot, *kalguksu* (knife-cut noodle soup), and *tteokguk* (rice cake soup). You can use it as a base for baby food and drink it instead of water for weight loss, as it makes you feel full. You can also eat the cooked kelp leftover after making stock, simply seasoning it with some soy sauce, sesame, and salt. Seasoned kelp can also be used as a topping for soups. Kelp powder is used frequently in *japchae* and dishes that use starch.

Shiitake Mushroom

Shiitake stock adds savory flavor to a dish and enhances its scent. It's rich in vitamin D, making it good for preventing osteoporosis, fatigue, and hypertrophy of the heart. It also contains vitamins B1 and B2, which help reduce canker sores and inflammation of the lips. Vitamin B6 helps with skin disease and anemia. In the West, shiitake mushrooms are called "the food of the gods" and a "miracle food" for their abundance of calcium, iron, and magnesium, as well as the anticarcinogenic lentinan and methionine, which clear the head.

To prepare, rinse the dried mushrooms under running water and simmer them for an hour or two. To get a richer broth, place it in the shade or fridge for a day. Afterward, you can stir-fry the mushrooms used for the broth with some sesame seeds or make *jeon* pancakes.

Shiitake mushrooms are low in calories, making them a popular diet food. You can see optimal health outcomes by drinking water brewed with shiitake and kelp. However, this fungus is not suitable for people who have gout. Shiitake goes well with other ingredients and can be used in soup, stew, steamed dishes, and with *doenjang* and *gochujang* in dishes like *bibimbap*. Broth made with shiitake and kelp is often used in temples. To prepare, boil the kelp and shiitake, add soy sauce, and continue to let boil.

Shiitakes are best used in soup-based dishes or added to *doenjang*-based dishes to enhance their scent and flavor.

Black and White Beans

Black beans are called a "super black food" for their properties, including flavonoids, anthocyanin, and isoflavone, which make them effective for blood circulation and anti-aging. The lecithin in black beans acts as a detoxifier and anticarcinogen and helps purify the blood, lower cholesterol, and remove toxins. Vitamins B1 and B12 help prevent hair loss, stimulate hair growth, and smoothen the skin. Amino acids like lysine and tryptophan help to keep the body warm. Black beans also boost virility, help with sexual dysfunction, and stimulate breast milk production. Pureed white soybeans can be added to soup, steamed dishes, or flour-based foods for extra protein.

These beans are simple to prepare. First, rinse the soaked beans under running water and place them in a pot. Cover the beans with water, filling the pot, and then boil them with the lid off. After ten minutes, skim the froth from the boiling water. Wait for the beans to cool, then grind them. Make a bunch to store in the fridge and use whenever needed. You can make a braising sauce by boiling regular soy sauce with black beans, shiitake mushrooms, kelp, and ginger. You can also grind the beans into a fine powder after roasting them and removing their skin. The powder can be added to soup, spring vegetables, or water for a summer noodle dish.

Cinnamon Powder

Cinnamon is a spice that's sweet, sour, and spicy. In the West, its sweetness was used as a symbol of love. Cinnamon powder is made by drying and grinding the thin bark of a cassia tree. It must be sealed tightly and stored in a dry area. In Western dishes, it's often used in desserts like cake, pudding, and cookies. In Korea, it's used to make sweet potato and chestnut rice balls, *yakgwa* (sweet wheat-based snack) and fruit-and-cinnamon punch. Cinnamon powder can be added to food to give it a pleasant scent. Drinking it in tea with ginger powder is also beneficial for fever, circulation, sweating, and boosting energy. Cinnamon clears the head and nose and helps to calm an anxious mind. Mixing cinnamon extract in warm water to use as toothpaste can also prevent germs and bad breath.

Seed Powder

Perilla and sesame seed powder are often used in vegetable salads, soups, stews, and steamed dishes. To make perilla seed powder, wash and dry the seeds thoroughly before roasting them in a pan. Grind the roasted seeds and use them straight away or strain them. Perilla powder oxidizes fast at room temperature, so you must seal it properly and store it in the freezer to preserve its scent and taste. It's often used with rice powder because perilla seeds lack viscosity. Unlike sesame seeds, perilla seeds are a warm food, so eating them for a long time can cure coldness. If you have cold hands and feet, stir the seeds in honey and drink a cup or two as tea every day to make your body warm and improve your complexion. You can also make a low-calorie porridge by grinding water-soaked glutinous rice and boiling it with perilla seed powder.

According to *Dongui Bogam*, perilla seeds warm the body, calm the mind, and stop coughs and phlegm. They are a warm food containing insoluble fiber, helping suppress breast and colorectal cancer. They contain  a lot of vitamin E, which improves eyesight, prevents gout, and boosts reproductive functions. The omega-3 fatty acids stimulate the brain's nerves and help prevent dementia.

Sesame seeds are an indispensable ingredient for making sauce, as their scent is a palate stimulant. They've been used throughout the ages all over the world and carry a mysterious magic—like the phrase "open sesame" in the story *Ali Baba and the Forty Thieves*. There's a Korean expression, "You can catch up with a running horse if you eat sesame seeds." This speaks to sesame's ability to provide energy. Drinking it as tea can strengthen a weak constitution, improve anemia and lack of energy, help with rough skin, and get rid of tinnitus and other symptoms of aging.

The linoleic acid in sesame seeds is effective for improving memory, preventing dementia and aging, treating various brain diseases, and curing a hangover. Sesame seeds also have a lot of oleic acid, which helps to prevent arterial stiffness and maintain elasticity. To make sesame seed tea, peel the outer skin, roast until you can smell the scent, grind them finely, and add a bit of salt. A good ratio is one cup of boiling water and one tablespoon of sesame seed powder to drink once or twice daily. Sesame seed powder goes well with all kinds of food, including salads and potato pancakes. Their high caloric content made them an emergency food in ancient times.

Pine needle powder is also used in temple cuisine to add flavor. It has a strong, bitter taste, so adding a little bit to stir-fried dishes or soup goes a long way.

To harvest, pine needles are gathered early in the morning, washed under running water, and then dried. Grind them into a powder, boil in low heat, and drink it sweetened with honey. You can also mix pine needle powder, black bean powder, black sesame powder, honey, and water to drink twice or three times daily for three weeks. Adding pine needle powder to yogurt daily will significantly lower your blood pressure. Pine needle extract can be made to use in tea or other foods. To do so, alternate layers of pine and honey in a vat, add water, seal it tightly, and store it in a cool, shaded spot to ripen. After one hundred days, you can take it out and drink it as tea. You can also soften the extract's scent and taste by removing the pine needles and allowing the mixture to age longer. You can also make pine lotus porridge by grinding lotus root and adding pine needle extract.

The primary components of pine needles are terpene and tannin. Tannin blocks iron absorption, so pregnant women shouldn't eat pine needles. However, pine needles contain glycogen, which helps with diabetes, and lutein, which strengthens the capillary vessel. They're also packed with iron, which helps with anemia, and other healthy minerals and components like chlorophyll, beta-carotene, vitamin B complex, and vitamin C.

Green Tea Powder

Green tea is made by pausing fermentation on delicate roasted leaves. It's important to make it without destroying the vitamin C. Its unique and bitter taste is due to catechins like tannin. The sweetness comes from amino acids, and the scent results from an interaction between alcohols and organic acids. The caffeine in green tea acts as a diuretic and momentarily eases fatigue by stimulating the brain. It also energizes the muscles, controls blood flow, and lowers cholesterol and blood pressure. It helps digestion by stimulating the stomach and quickening the release of gastric fluids. It's excellent at dissecting fat and suppressing bacterial growth.

Green tea powder is great on its own as a sweetener but is also used to add vibrant color to foods like noodles, rice cakes, pancakes, and steamed dishes. However, consuming green tea for a long time can cause coldness, so it's best to steep it in hot water for a brief time and avoid reusing the tea.

Honey and Rice Syrup

Like water, honey gets absorbed by the body through osmotic pressure. So, it's best to use a relatively weak honey. Honey contains many minerals and nutrients and is sensitive to heat, so it must be left raw and added as the final step to a dish to avoid destroying the nutrients. It provides sweetness and nutrition to salads and tea.

Rice syrup (*jocheong*) is a traditional, natural sweetener made by simmering rice and malt for a long time. It's made without bleaching or refinement processes, so the nutrients from the rice remain active, but the flavor, scent, and color become quite potent, making it essential to use the right portion. Its high viscosity suits stir-fried dishes like *tteokbokki* (stir-fried spicy rice cakes) and candied sweet potatoes. Other natural sweeteners include agave syrup, maple syrup, and fruit extract.

Mountain Herb Extract

Mountain herb extract is a flavoring that requires more patience than *doenjang*, soy sauce, and pickles. The herbs must be gathered in a clean area at the appropriate time. Depending on the species of mountain herb, there's a different time for harvest and a variety of methods for preparing the herbs. Mountain herb must then be placed in storage pots at the right moment before fermenting. While it takes a long time to make, this extract adds the bounty and flavor of nature to any recipe in which it is included. You can add mountain herb extract to salads or put it in tea to receive the skin care, hormonal growth, digestion, and immunity benefits of the kalium, calcium, and natural minerals in mountain herb.

If it's too difficult to make an herb extract, you can make herb vinegar by aging the stems and roots with sugar, yeast, and glutinous rice. For a more manageable process, pour brown rice vinegar onto the herbs. Herbal vinegar can be used in various salads. In temple food, vinegar is often made with lemon, ginseng, black raspberries, goji berries, and other fruits. Vinegar contains many components that dissect fat in the blood, so herbal vinegar gives more variety to food and promotes well-being.

Fruit and Vegetable Soy Sauce

To make a vegetable soy sauce, start by boiling vegetables like radishes, lettuce, carrots, or onions. Add black beans and continue to boil. Add soy sauce or salt to taste and boil on medium heat. Once the sauce is reduced, allow it to cool before straining the vegetables. Store the vegetable soy sauce in the fridge for use in cooking. To make a fruit-vegetable soy sauce, follow the same process, adding fruits like apples, oranges, or lemons.

Vegetable Stock

To make a vegetable stock, place large slices of radish in water alongside shiitake and kelp and bring to a boil. Add lettuce, cabbage, carrots, mushrooms—any leftover vegetables you have on hand are suitable. This stock is an excellent base for any soup dish. It can also be added to baby food to help infants become acquainted with the taste of vegetables.

Temple *Ganjang* (Soy Sauce)

Salt, *doenjang*, *ganjang*, and *gochujang* are the basic seasonings of a temple's cuisine. At Guemsuam Temple, we use homemade soy sauce or braising soy sauce (*jorimganjang*) instead of store-bought. To make braising soy sauce, start with a stock made with kelp and shiitake mushrooms, add two cups of black beans, and boil. Then, strain the solids. Mix this with a standard soy sauce for lighter, braising soy sauce. To achieve a sour taste, add a splash of vinegar. Depending on the desired salt level, you can dilute the sauce with broth or water as needed.

Temple Sauces

Temple food is so simple and natural that discussing "sauce" may sound out of place. But when it comes to a vegetarian diet, incorporating various sauces is necessary for developing flavor. Adding sauce to vegetables, nuts, and fruits gives them a more bountiful taste. Nature-based sauces also provide the means to enjoy food slowly with ease and delicacy. Temples are always full of vegetables and fruits. Sauces are usually added to give variety. Mixing tofu, nuts, olive oil, salt, vinegar, and celery gives you a basic vegetarian sauce, but it's important not to use too many nuts to avoid an unpleasant texture. For instance, the added walnuts, pine nuts, and peanuts shouldn't exceed one spoonful. It's also okay to add pumpkin or sunflower seeds.

Basic Vegetarian Sauce

You can make basic vegetarian sauce by mixing tofu, nuts, olive oil, salt, and celery. First, blanch the tofu in boiling water for about five minutes and strain it to dry. Then add the tofu, two walnuts, a tablespoon of pine nuts and peanuts, a bit of celery, a tablespoon of olive oil, a teaspoon of salt, and a tablespoon of vinegar into a blender. This sauce can be used as salad dressing or on bread and pizza. For a sauce that complements vegetable or fruit salads, finely grind roasted seeds, smash the slightly blanched tofu, and mix them with soy milk, lemon extract, salt, and white pepper. To make a sauce with silken tofu, use a block of tofu, one green pepper, fifty grams of parsley, one tablespoon of lemon juice, and a bit of salt. This can be used as a simple, fresh base for all dishes. Adjusting the portion of tofu or beans can give you a wider variety of textures and flavors.

Fruit Sauce

Orange sauce is made from the entire fruit by grinding the skin and juicing the pulp before adding whipped cream and basic vegetarian sauce. The orange in the sauce can be replaced with tangerine, yuzu, or other citrus fruits and complements salads.

Strawberries are another fruit that can be added to the vegetarian sauce with whipped cream.

All a simple kiwi sauce requires is freshly ground kiwi with a bit of salt added. Pears and bananas are other fruits that can be mixed with salt to form a sauce.

Melon can also be ground, boiled down, and added to a basic vegetarian sauce to provide a sweet and mild flavor.

Tomato Sauce

Tomato sauce follows a cooking process similar to fruit sauce. Remove any stems before placing the tomato in boiling water. Once it's boiled, remove it from the water, peel it, and slice it. Boil the peeled tomato before blending it with other ingredients.

Chestnut Sauce

To make a chestnut sauce, steam the chestnut, peel the skin, and smash the pulp. Blend the chestnut pulp with tofu, various dried fruits and nuts, vinegar, and salt to taste. You can also grind raw chestnuts, boil them well, and add a bit of rice syrup to make a wonderful sauce that goes well with rice cake, dumplings, cookies, and bread.

Ginkgo Sauce

Blend ginkgo nuts with tofu, kiwi, dried fruits and nuts, olive oil, salt, and vinegar to make a nutritious and fresh sauce. Roasted salted ginkgos are enjoyed as a snack or topping, but they can also be made into a sauce by following the steps above.

Bean Sauce

To make a black bean sauce, softened beans can be blended with soy milk, salt, and olive oil. Mixing them with black sesame seeds gives you a highly nutritious sauce that helps with anti-aging, disease prevention, and weight loss. You can also make a sauce from white beans by adding pumpkin seeds and a bit of salt.

Wild Greens Sauce

To make a wild greens sauce, simply add the greens to a basic vegetarian sauce. Adding bellflower root will make a salad dressing. For a bitter taste, add a pinch of mugwort powder. Adding yogurt to the greens makes a flavorful, tasty sauce.

Black Bean Soy Sauce

Black bean soy sauce goes well with boiled or roasted dishes. To make, first, wash and dry the beans thoroughly. Rinse dried shiitake mushrooms and kelp as well. Pour water into a pot, put in the beans, and boil them for twenty minutes. Add the other ingredients and boil for seven more minutes. Remove the shiitake and kelp, add some soy sauce, and boil for an additional minute. If you add equal amount of soy sauce and rice syrup then simmer, you can make teriyaki sauce.

Goji Berry Soy Sauce

To prepare a goji berry sauce, heat a pan and add goji berries with two tablespoons of *soju*. Simmer for seven minutes over medium heat, ensuring it doesn't burn. To cool quickly, place the sauce in a cold, windy area. Repeat this process nine times. Next, pour water into a pot, add shiitake mushrooms and kelp, then boil for seven more minutes. Strain the ingredients, add soy sauce, and boil for another minute. The finished sauce can be added to mountain herb rolls, mushroom dishes, and pancakes or eaten with dried seaweed to enhance the flavor. Store the sauce in a fridge and consume it within a few days. It's best to make the sauce base strong and dilute it according to the needs of a particular dish.

Cabbage Rice Rolls with Beet & Yuzu Doenjang Sauce

(Baechu Beet Bap & Yuja Doenjang Sauce)

Nutritious napa cabbages with a subtle, sweet flavor are perfect for making rice rolls. Napa cabbages harvested in late fall *kimchi*-making season are a popular ingredient at temples because fall cabbages keep well until late spring. The savory *doenjang* sauce mixed with yuzu gives uniquely delicious flavors to the cabbage. Beets are usually used in a juice form, as a natural coloring, or in salads. These cabbage rolls were created to encourage more usage of beets. They are a nice change from *kimbap* or other rice rolls and an excellent option for lunch boxes.

Ingredients

¾ cup (about 7 ounces) uncooked short-grain rice

5 to 6 napa cabbage leaves

3 to 4 shiitake mushrooms

¼ *danhobak* (kabocha squash), peeled

¼ beet, peeled

Salt, *gukganjang* (soup soy sauce), sesame oil for seasoning

Sauce:

½ small potato, peeled

½ cup mushroom broth (boil water with a small piece of dried kelp, about 2 inches, and a dried shiitake mushroom for a few minutes)

1 tablespoon *doenjang*

1 teaspoon *jocheong* (rice syrup)

1 tablespoon *yuja-cheong* (yuzu marmalade)

Directions

1. Cook the rice using a little less water than usual to make it fluffy.

2. Blanch the napa cabbage leaves in salted boiling water, then rinse in cold water and squeeze out the water.

3. Julienne the shiitake mushrooms, season lightly with soup soy sauce and sesame oil, and briefly pan-fry.

4. Use a mandoline to julienne the squash, then lightly pan-fry in sesame oil. Season lightly with soup soy sauce.

5. Julienne the beet and soak in cold water to remove some of its red color. Drain, mix with a pinch of salt, and set aside. A few minutes later, squeeze out the water, then pan-fry lightly in sesame oil.

6. Lay flat a prepared napa cabbage leaf lengthwise, and spread some rice on top. Add the prepared vegetables and roll up like you would for a *kimbap* roll.

7. To make the sauce, grate the potato or blend it in a mini food processor. Boil the mushroom broth with *doenjang*, and add the grated potato, rice syrup and yuzu marmalade. Simmer for a minute or two to finish the sauce.

8. Slice the cabbage rice rolls into bite-sized pieces, and serve with the sauce on the side.

Lettuce Wrap with Burdock Root & Soy Protein

(Ueong Kongsalmari & Sangchu Ssam)

Burdock roots and soybeans have nutritional compounds that help boost energy and stamina. Green lettuce helps improve the quality of sleep. This dish can provide a moment of restfulness for those who are living busy, modern lives. This recipe transforms these ingredients into a harmonious meal.

Ingredients

1 *ueong* (burdock) root

7 ounces soy meat

½ cup *chapssal garu* (sweet rice flour/glutinous rice flour)

½ cup potato starch

½ cup water

Oil for frying

Seasoning for soy meat:

1 teaspoon *gukganjang* (soup soy sauce)

1 tablespoon sesame oil

Coating sauce:

2 tablespoons regular soy sauce

1 tablespoon *maesilcheong* (green plum syrup)

Ssamjang (dipping sauce):

1 tablespoon *doenjang*

1 tablespoon *maesilcheong* (green plum syrup)

1 tablespoon sesame seeds

Vegetable wraps:

7 ounces green or red leaf lettuce

10 *kkaennip* (perilla) leaves

Directions

1. Cut the burdock root lengthwise into 3-inch pieces, and steam them. Once cooled, flatten them by gently pounding down with a wooden mallet.
2. Season the soy meat with the soup soy sauce and sesame oil.
3. Place the soy meat on a flattened burdock root, and roll it up. Repeat for all the pieces.
4. Make a batter with the sweet rice flour, potato starch, and water.
5. Dip the rolled burdock roots in the batter, and fry them until golden brown.
6. Bring the coating sauce ingredients to a boil, then toss the fried rolls in the sauce.
7. Mix together the ingredients for the *ssamjang* (dipping sauce).
8. Serve the fried rolls with the vegetable wraps along with the dipping sauce.

Grilled Mushrooms in Sweet Rice Batter

(Seogi Beoseot Chapssal Gui)

Seogi beoseot (rock tripe mushrooms/lichens) grow on large boulders and rocks that sit deep in the mountains. They are full of anti-cancer and restorative properties and used as traditional medicine for improving chronic ailments, such as blood pressure and blood sugar. Rock tripe mushrooms are even better than *neungi beoseot* (shingled hedgehog mushrooms), known as the number one medicinal mushroom in Korea. While shingled hedgehogs grow fully in one year, rock tripe mushrooms only grow one millimeter in one year. To reach the size of a palm, it could take seventy to eighty years. Thus, it is a quite special mushroom.

Ingredients

2 ounces *seogi beoseot* (rock tripe mushrooms/lichens) or *mogi beoseot* (wood ear mushrooms)
2 tablespoons *chapssal garu* (sweet rice flour/glutinous rice flour)
Sesame oil

Marinade:
1 tablespoon regular soy sauce
1 tablespoon *jocheong* (rice syrup)
½ cup kelp water (1 small piece dried kelp boiled in ¾ cup water for 5 minutes)

1. Quickly blanch the rock tripe mushrooms in boiling water, then rinse repeatedly to remove any remaining dirt.

2. Remove the hard stem section of the mushrooms, which are too tough to eat.

3. Briefly boil the marinade ingredients, and then marinate the mushrooms for an hour.

4. Remove the mushrooms and dredge each mushroom piece in the sweet rice flour.

5. Add a small amount of sesame oil to a non-stick pan and lightly wipe the pan with a paper towel to distribute the oil. Grill the mushrooms on both sides until the sweet rice flour coating is lightly golden brown.

part four

A Sharing Table

Although temple cuisine has its origins in Buddhism, there was nothing known as "temple cuisine" during the time of the Buddha. In those days, temple food was simply any food the temple received as alms that was shared evenly among the monks. This practice of asking for alms is called *Pindapata* and was passed down as a Buddhist ritual—a way to provide an opportunity for people to make an offering. Since food was acquired through the donation of alms, there wasn't an opportunity for any development of a Buddhist food culture. Spending time on the basic necessities of life—like food and drink—was thought to distract from practice, so *Pindapata* was conducted for a long period of time among Buddhist monks.

In Southeast Asian countries like Sri Lanka, Myanmar, Thailand, and Cambodia, this practice of giving alms still exists, so there is no concept of a separate temple cuisine. Those who take care of the temples cook food, including fish, and share it with the monks. There are no boundaries or guiding principles for food like those in Korean temple cuisine.

Instead, as Buddhism from northern India spread throughout Southeast Asia, separate temple cultures and temple food practices were developed. In Tibet, the nomadic tribal culture dominates, and even the monks consume yak tea and meat. Except for a few special occasions, it's rare to eat a completely vegetarian diet in Tibet. Bhutan is a Buddhist country but imports meat from India and Nepal. In Chinese temples, they cook simple, clean food and don't use the Five Pungent Plants (garlic, scallion, onion, *buchu*/garlic chives, and *dalrae*/small wild onions). Food is usually made by the female monks, and the male monks take care of the outside chores. While maintaining separate lodging, female and male monks live and practice together.

According to Dōgen Zenji, the founder of the Sōtō school of Zen Buddhism, Buddhism first spread to Japan during the Baekje Kingdom.[1] Since the Kamakura period (1180-1333), Japanese temple food has been considered the "food of practice." Dōgen stressed the importance of everyday practice and considered everything in daily life to be a part of that practice, especially food. This greatly affected the dietary culture in Japan, which didn't have sophisticated cooking methods at the time. Dōgen's teachings led to a culinary revolution and the development of various cooking methods using soy sauce and *doenjang* (miso). In present-day Japanese food practices, temple food is sold in standard restaurants. In Japan, famous temples are full of visitors who want to try this "food of practice"—temple food—similar to how our temple food restaurant, Balwoo Gongyang, is located in front of the Jogyesa Temple in Seoul.

Buddhism spread throughout Korea in 372 during the Goguryeo Kingdom under King Sosurim. Then, even kings abstained from hunting during festival periods and faced restrictions on killing livestock. This tradition and temple food culture were passed down until the Goryeo period (918-1392). But there was nothing hierarchical or novel about temple food. It was merely food made by people who were poor and cooked simply, according to the wisdom of nature.

Then, Confucianism arrived in Korea via China, bringing with it a culture of meat consumption. Confucian practice includes preparing meals for dead ancestors that feature meat, alcohol, and spices. Since then, meat consumption has firmly taken hold in Korea's popular food culture. After the Joseon Dynasty's open-door policy and in the aftermath of the Korean

1 Baekje Kingdom (18 BCE – 660 CE) was one of the ancient Korean kingdoms during Three Kingdom Period.

War, the availability of instant and meat-based food began to grow with abandon. The traditional practices of temple food grew increasingly distant from the people. Ironically, temple cuisine is now considered a special food culture of its own.

What Is Temple Food?

Simply put, temple food is the food eaten by Buddhist monks in their daily practice. It's made without using meat or the Five Pungent Plants and Spices forbidden by the Buddha. These days, temple cuisine is drawing attention from layfolk as a safe and healthy diet. As those who begin to eat temple food consistently notice their quality of life improve, the desire to continue to live and eat well also increases. This leads to an emphasis on a plant-based diet and, therefore, temple food. But temple food shines brightest when it is shared among many at the same table and cooked with minimal labor or pain inflicted on others. How we eat is equally as important as what we eat. Healthy living requires the right amount of exercise and a proper diet. This is not possible without a strong will. Temple food embodies Buddhist philosophy and culture and provides quality taste, nutrition, and strength of mind and body. It is the food of wisdom that reflects the values of Buddhism and clears the spirit.

The Food of the World vs. The Food of Practice

In Buddhism, food is defined according to the questions: who, what, when, where, why, and how. If it's eaten by regular people, it's the food of the people. If it's consumed by monks, it's the food of practitioners.

In the *Āgama Sutras*, the Buddha talks about four kinds of foods: *dansik, choksik, sasik,* and *siksik* (단식, 초식, 사식, 식식). *Dansik* (edible food) refers to rough, lumped, thick and thin, and tasty food. It's any food we can put inside our mouths and chew. *Choksik* (food of sensations) is the food of sense impressions. It speaks of various scents, flowers, texture, delicate pleasure, and food sensations. *Sasik* (food of volition) is food in the realm of abstract thoughts, memories, will, and intention that we deliver through our mouths and feel with our bodies. *Siksik* (food of consciousness) is the food we can only know through our hearts and minds. The Buddha said if there are emotions like greed and happiness in these four kinds of foods, there's also sadness and worry, blemish and dirt. If there's no greed or happiness, then there's no sadness or worry and no blemish or dirt. This means a clean, untainted diet of temple food can lead to the enlightenment by maintaining a pure mind and body.

Cleanliness of *dansik* is achieved by preparing ingredients according to their rightful nature and avoiding contamination of the foods we consume directly with our mouths. Cleanliness of *choksik* means cooking with an egalitarian mind without being trapped by the senses or the three poisons of *tam, jin, and chi*. Cleanliness of *sasik* means removing any attachments and cultivating compassion and peaceful benevolence in our food. Cleanliness of *siksik* means not allowing even the tiniest speck of dust in our consciousness and honoring the virtue of purity with clear insight. It's achieved through learning the value of emptiness and consuming the food of wisdom. If our food is unclean, we will continue to be trapped in a cycle of death and rebirth by consuming these four types of food.

The Buddha also spoke of five types of food for practicing disciples. The first is the food of *seon*, the wisdom of seeing everything in existence as one. The second is the food of *won*, the power to bring forth our wishes and intentions. The third is the food of *yeom*, the wisdom of staying true to our practice by always keeping it in our thoughts. The fourth is the food of nirvana's enlightenment. The fifth is the food of joy.

The practice of begging for alms helps disciples to avoid food tainted by the world and maintain a pure diet. Temple food can be considered a culinary culture that transcends the four concepts of food and instead encourages the consumption of oneness, intention, mindfulness, enlightenment, and joy. Contemporary temple cuisine also embraces eating with the joy of enlightenment rather than polluting our minds and bodies with worldly food.

The Food of Nature and Restraint

During the time of the Buddha, there were no special limitations on food, as meals were taken once a day through alms. But as time passed, rules started forming around the food of the disciples, such as the restriction of meat. These teachings are contained in the *Dharmaguptaka* and include eating according to the time of day and seasons, embracing diversity, avoiding excess, and limiting meat.

Eating in accordance with time originally referred to refraining from eating food after midday, as animals eat in the afternoon and spirits eat at night. But a broader definition can look like porridge in the morning, a light lunch with rice and three types of *banchan*, and fruit in the evening. In the morning, eating porridge is good for avoiding troubling the stomach and helping the brain function. The Buddha suggested porridge to his disciples. The *Mahāsāṃghika Vinaya* speaks of ten different benefits of porridge, including brightening the complexion, providing energy and comfort, lengthening life, freshening the voice, protecting against the cold, filling the stomach, quenching thirst, and balancing urine and stool. Travelers to India can find a variety of porridge for sale on the streets. Though the portions are small, they're enough to be filling.

In the afternoon, there's an abundance of sunlight and increased activity, so it's good to eat hard food or a proper meal that can support the mind and body. Meals taken in the evening should aid the digestion and release of food consumed during the day. Eating outside these hours breaks the rhythmic flow of the meals and may affect one's practice, so eating at the proper times of the day is best.

Eating seasonally used to be instinctual and obvious, but today, there are so many frozen foods that our tables are full of out-of-season ingredients. Because an ingredient's nutrients and benefits differ depending on the season, it's best to eat seasonally and locally to receive the most benefit for our bodies. Each human body is like a small universe that is affected by the twenty-four solar terms of the year. Our organs receive nutrients differently based on the season, so eating fresh, unprocessed, seasonal produce is incredibly important.

Embracing diversity refers to receiving nutrients through various ingredients. But diversity here doesn't mean eating all kinds of food as one would at a buffet. Rather, it means eating in alignment with the five elemental phases, even if there are only three ingredients, and avoiding excess or lack. Overeating subjects the body to extreme stress and harm. Once the body gets used to this, the mind also fills with greed and can become constantly anxious and dissatisfied. Overeating is like a dark lion that wears a false mask of abundance while destroying the mind and body.

Similarly, eating meat must be limited unless a person needs it. The most important precept in Buddhism is *ahimsa*—not harming life. This idea includes respect for all living things and carries the principle of great benevolence. In the *Brahmajāla Sūtra*, the Buddha says, "All bodhisattvas

must refrain from eating meat. Eating meat is a great sin, and those who eat meat have tainted what is pure." In other words, we should refrain from eating meat since all living creatures are our close relations. Eating meat also fills animals with fear and makes those around us lose faith. Since we are all one with nature, animals value their lives just as much as we value ours. Therefore, harming a precious life that lives and breathes as we do, for selfish reasons, is an incredibly violent act. That's why the Buddha tells us to avoid a meat-based diet.

The Evolution of Vegetarian and Medicinal Food

Some faiths practice praying for blessings. However, some prominent religious organizations in Buddhism and Christianity view this as a distorted faith. Buddhism is not a religion of blessings. Still, during the Joseon era, temples had a hard time surviving. So, at that time, people brought their offerings to the temples along with their worries and prayed for blessings. Their prayers were sent up into the sky as light, and their wishes created a ripple in the universe. Pure prayers help to grant the wish of the one who is praying. The saying, "Heaven helps those who help themselves," isn't just a phrase. But as it isn't always easy for people to pray with care and sincerity, the bigger their concern, the more they wish for the support of monks.

Monks have been practicing fervently at dawn since ancient times, but people haven't always had a chance to witness this. Even if lay folk knew how to practice, it was impossible to do so while caring for their families and struggling to survive. So, when they came to the temple, they spent more time praying than learning how to practice. At times, the monks added to their prayers. Because of this, people started to wish for an influential monk's prayers and made offerings in earnest. During the time of the Buddha, many people brought him their troubles as well. Each time, the Buddha gave them the wisdom and insight to resolve their troubles on their own. Thus, Buddhism is closer to a religion of support and assistance.

But since the Joseon era, monks have had to pray with the people to maintain the temples. Due to this tradition, modern Buddhism now includes an element of praying for blessings, even though initially, Korean Buddhism was a practice-based faith seeking to transcend all texts and achieve enlightenment through self-reflection. The practice passed down since the Shilla era is called *Seon,*[2] and the primary order of Zen Buddhism is the Jogye Order. *Seon* has flowed to us like water since the time of the Buddha, and temple cuisine is a sacred practice that upholds this tradition. It is the food of gratitude, benevolence, and enlightenment.

Vegetarian food is any cuisine that doesn't contain meat. Its definition is broad, which means out-of-season ingredients can also be considered vegetarian. Even veganism cannot wholly exclude instant foods like ramen, chips, and other processed foods. However, vegetarianism, at its core, is rooted in the philosophy of respect for all life. Its practitioners seek to love their neighbors and the earth. Even if some people may practice a vegetarian diet simply for their health, beauty, or taste preferences, it's still better than a meat-based diet. But upon more self-reflection, many will find it natural to embrace a vegetarian diet, not just out of need or duty.

Food doesn't always act like medicine, even if all life contains healing properties. But at times, a balanced diet may provide more benefits than

---

2 Zen Buddhism

medicine. Medicinal food has become quite popular in contemporary culture—rooted in the belief that food and medicine stem from the same source. But healing cuisine also makes use of medicinal herbs and ingredients like tortoise shells, bear feet and bladder, and centipede. Based on herbal medicine, it allows the medical properties of the food to well up and pour out through the animal ingredients. A common example of this is *samgye-tang*, or ginseng chicken soup. When combined with animal ingredients, the medical properties of plants add a soothing effect. They are indispensable for releasing toxins from an animal and bringing out their healing properties.

Medical food is needed for an illness, but it's not good to seek it out based on an erroneous preference. Eating too much of it can confuse the body, enhancing one part while weakening another. Living a life centered around the strong part can make the weak part fatal. But you don't see this happening with temple food, which harmonizes the mind and body. Common plants and herbs undergo a self-purification process, giving us peace, fragrance, and strength.

The Art of a Light Diet

A lean diet is the hallmark of temple food—the practice of eating minimally to curb desire and appreciate life. To exaggerate a little, those who eat a lot are harming a lot of life. At the temple, we express gratitude for the minimal amount of food and do our best daily to return the favors offered to us. A student must learn the basics necessary to become a part of society, an employee must use their skills to benefit the company and culture, and a household must cook food efficiently to enable all parties to fulfill their societal duties. This is the price of food as determined by fate.

The Five Pungent Plants are garlic, scallion, onion, *buchu* (garlic chives), and *dalrae* (small wild onions) in Korean Temple cuisine. These are necessary ingredients for cooking and are known to benefit the body, providing stamina and medicinal properties. The Five Pungent Plants are good ingredients that provide yang energy, but if a person with excess body heat eats too much of them, they can suffer from a heat rash. Even good ingredients don't benefit everyone, so we can't only consider the nutritional properties.

The *Śūraṅgama Sūtra* says, "Beings who seek *samadhi* should refrain from eating five pungent plants of this world. If these five are eaten cooked, they increase one's sexual desire; if they are eaten raw, they increase one's anger." Eating the Five Pungent Plants distracts the mind, builds anger, and leads one to a non-disciplinary life. Early texts don't mention them. Based on their mentions in the *Nirvana Sūtra*, *Brahmajāla Sūtra*, and the *Fayuan Zhulin*,[3] some believe the teaching comes from Mahayana Buddhism or China. The Five Pungent Plants all carry strong scents, which could have been forbidden as they can disturb others and distract one from practice. Too much yang energy can disrupt the flow or stimulate excess sweat, which can stink. So, avoiding the five plants is one way to find peace of mind. For students, job seekers, and those fervently wishing for a specific result, I suggest gaining energy from ingredients with a fresh scent. We can receive energy from a pure heart and mind, so avoiding stimulants can help. The intense yang energy in the five plants can be compared to things that disturb the peace of mind and body.

When we have too much or too little energy, we create clots. This grows even fiercer when one is experiencing a strong obsession. These things

---

3 A Chinese Buddhist encyclopedia dating back to 668

build anguish, and the Five Pungent Plants can stimulate the mind further. This causes us to live in constant anxiety and clouds the mind's eye. A mind trapped in these false beliefs can create a life of suffering. So, we must remember that even an obsession with health can make us unhappy.

But if we can eliminate any greed for the Five Pungent Plants, they can be used as beneficial ingredients. In the *Fayuan Zhulin*, the Buddha permits eating garlic for seven days for a sick monk who can't be cured otherwise. But he also prescribes eating it in the corner of a small room, avoiding lying in public areas or on shared mats afterward, and refraining from visiting public restrooms or lecture halls. And after seven days, he must bathe and clothe properly before rejoining the public. This shows that the five plants are permitted for the sick, just like meat can be allowed for illness. The practice simply must not disturb those around the patient.

So, are the Five Pungent Plants a source of energy or the start of desire? They are a food of choice that we must take only after listening to our own clear, bright hearts.

From Our Tables to the World

In Buddhism, a meal is called *gongyang* (공양), or an offering. Everything we offer is called *gongyang*. Food is an offering of life to sustain the body. Calling food *gongyang* helps us remember the Buddha's teachings. It reminds us to thank nature for her kindness. Balwoo Gongyang, the name of our restaurant, refers to the practice of taking meals as an offering three times a day. It is a sacred practice of a devotee seeking enlightenment with every meal. *Bal* comes from the Sanskrit word, *pātra*, which is a vessel. *Woo* is the Chinese character for "bowl." So *Balwoo* refers to an alms bowl carrying the appropriate amount of food for each person.

The first meal offered to the Buddha after he sat under the Bodhi tree for six years and attained enlightenment came from the two merchants, Tapussa and Bhallika, who were carrying precious goods on 500 carts. When the Four Devas[4] knelt to worship, they placed flowers from the sky onto four stone bowls as an offering for the Buddha. Upon receiving this, the Buddha stacked the four bowls into one. The tradition of *balwoo gongyang* was born of the Buddha's first meal after enlightenment.

Balwoo isn't just a bowl for carrying food but a tool of enlightenment. In the story of *Aṅgulimāla*, the violent brigand becomes a disciple of the Buddha after receiving his teachings. The next day, Aṅgulimāla goes out with a bowl seeking alms. Originally, Aṅgulimāla's name was Ahimsa, which means nonviolence. But his foolishness led him to kill ninety-nine

---

4 The four heavenly guardians in Buddhism

lives and make a necklace out of the bloody fingers of those he killed, garnering the name Aṅgulimāla: "finger necklace." Those who knew of his violent deeds feared him and did not fill his alms bowl, but in the end, he received an offering.

The Art of the Packed Lunch

There's a growing interest in food and meditation as we rethink how we look at health to include both mind and body. Many TV networks are making shows about temple food with that in mind. As I do the work of popularizing this cuisine by running a restaurant, I'm glad I get to invite people to a meal that doesn't cause any harm and carries the essence of nature. As everything originates in the temple, I can't deny that it gives me a special sense of mission and joy as a monk carrying on the tradition. That's why I keep holding onto the thread that enables me to grow closer to the masses. I'm constantly experimenting with new menus, studying food nutrition, and keeping up with my spiritual practice.

Mountain trekking at the monastic school carries the great inconvenience of having to pack a lot of food in advance. Because everyone is equal, the size of each lunch box must also be the same. Every lunch box contains pickled radish, rice, and a bottle of water. Sometimes, the monks leave on a long journey of prayers. Though we may stay in one place, we set off with a light load when it's time to leave, carrying a meal in our knapsack.

There was a time when it was part of my duties to pack lunch for a senior monk. One time, he went on a trip to India. I wrestled with what to pack and finally arrived at roasted *doenjang*. I kneaded the paste until it was smooth and added chili peppers and mushrooms, roasting them until they were dehydrated. Then, I dried this concoction in the shade and packed it in single portions to make it easier to eat. This way, it was possible to make *doenjang* stew just by adding a bit of hot water.

Packed lunches are just as useful and convenient at a temple as in the outer world. But there was no lunchbox culture in the 1960s and 1970s, so we needed to research and experiment to make a healthy, convenient, and nutritious packed lunch. Then, the market became dominated by delivery food and instant food filled with meat and condiments.

When I was young, packed lunches usually came with kimchi. At times, the juice would spill and cause a mess. Likewise, temple lunches didn't have a suitable container to hold all the food, giving rise to odd meals. Then, in the 1990s the quality of life improved, as did the variety of food. We could now make pizza dough with potatoes. Because I felt the need for conveniently packed temple lunches, I published twenty recipes in the book *Happy Picnic*. In it, I also introduced temples around Seoul that would make for a great field trip. The book led to a packed lunch exhibition, and in 2011, an annex was opened to the restaurant responsible for creating convenient lunches full of natural ingredients and flavors.

Temple Food's Popularity Around the World

Thanks to the efforts of a diplomat working at the OECD headquarters, the city of Jeonju hosted a Korean food seminar. A famous French food critic, Claude Lebey, happened to attend the seminar and embarked upon a food tour of Seoul afterward. He was over eighty years old at the time but full of vigor. He had a bit of time left before returning to France, and the opening of Balwoo Gongyang drew his attention. He was extremely observant of the connection between the shape and taste of food and asked some sharp questions. Later, he remarked that temple food is the best Korean food. Due to this connection, we opened a temple food restaurant at the Galeries Lafayette department store in Paris. It was my great honor and joy to open a Korean temple food restaurant on a terrace overlooking the streets of Paris. Friends and local associates in Paris cheered on the endeavor, saying it was a good development for the country. All the harsh memories of the past melted away like snow with the sound of their applause.

During this exciting time surrounding the newfound global popularity of temple food, the Australian chef Nick Flynn visited Guemsuam Temple for a temple stay. At the time, he was the head chef at the Sky Lounge restaurant at the InterContinental Hotel in Seoul. During his whole stay, he kept looking at me. He finally said he envied the furnace and cauldron in the middle of the beautiful landscape and that we could gather seasonal ingredients as we desired. It was strange for him to follow Buddhist practices like sitting on the floor in silence, but he said it was a pleasant unfamiliarity. As for temple food, he described it as supremely delicate, tasty, simple, unique, and perfectly beautiful. Looking into his blue eyes full of wonder and amazement, I felt a sense of purpose for my work and thought once more about what to do in the future. Nick laughed as he said he would try making beautiful temple food with plenty of respect for nature and an absence of additives. His comment made me realize how lucky we are at Guemsuam Temple to eat this food daily.

One time, the actor Richard Gere visited Balwoo Gongyang. Our team was a bit excited and concerned by the sudden visit of a famous Hollywood star. But he was a gentleman during the whole meal and made us all feel comfortable. He said he was running two restaurants in New York and was interested in opening an Asian restaurant, too. When the chief monk suggested a temple food restaurant, he smiled brightly and asked, "Could Dae-Ahn *Seunim* come help?" After the meal, he gladly obliged us by taking a photo and leaving a voice memo. Sadly, the latter was deleted due to poor technical skill, but the moment lives on in memory.

If food was once considered a necessity of life, we are now living in an era where food determines one's quality of life. Some people experience starvation due to a lack of food, while others suffer from diseases brought on by a greedy appetite. We are suffering from both lack and abundance of food. The increasing consumption of meat is bringing about more diseases and setting humanity backward in terms of respecting life. It's a relief that temple food can offer a peaceful solution. This is also the reason that temple food needs to be globalized. Many countries besides Korea don't have a lot of vegetarian restaurants. But once people see that our temple food is prepared with a love of peace and nature, carrying respect for all living things, they will embrace it in exchange for a more violent, meat-based diet. When the world sees that temple food is a healthy, peaceful diet that honors the mysterious tastes of nature, they will be captivated by its unique magic.

We first need a change in thought to change the food preferences of a modern society that prioritizes stimulating flavors. Many condiments contain chemicals that can cause illness when they enter the body because they can't be converted into nutrients as they're absorbed and digested. But temple food uses all the parts of a plant, from root to flower, and honors the nature of each ingredient, making it distinct from vegetarian

food. It is a beneficial diet that can help prevent aging and maintain youth and vitality for a long time so that we may live a life full of vigor.

K-Pop, K-Temple Food

The Jogye Order of Buddhism in Korea has held events worldwide to introduce temple food, including a lecture at the New York campus of the Culinary Institute of America, the ITB Berlin trade fair, and the Korean Cultural Center in Paris. Traveling the globe to lecture on temple food fills me with pride, hope, and a vision for what the future holds.

In 2010, we prepared a large feast for the New Yorkers attending a UN event for "Korean Temple Food Day." It was an international event attended by monks specializing in temple food, drawing much attention and praise.

In 2011, I attended the ITB fair in Germany. My schedule was busy, but I wasn't the least bit tired. Sharing our food and philosophy gave me great pleasure and happiness. The time I spent in Berlin was productive and informative. It was interesting to be with people who have a very different food culture. I was hopeful I'd discover an idea to expand the globalization of temple food by spending time with them. I was struck by the sight of the Germans heading out to the bakery in the market every morning, where our host went each day to fill the display with bread. The German bread didn't look particularly fancy, but it was fresh, tasty, and affordable.

At the fair, we held a food demo and tasting for an hour. Seeing men in suits waiting in line for over an hour to hear the lecture and taste our food was amusing. They were full of curiosity as they expressed their interest in temple cuisine. Our pickled rice wrap was popular, as well as the *minari* perilla seed stew and the salad with pine nut and *deodeok* dressing. The typical German diet consists of sausage and other meats served with sliced cabbage and fried in oil. I was sincerely concerned about the excess trans fat in their diet and filled with a newfound determination to develop more vegetarian dishes to repay their love and interest in our food.

After Germany, I visited France, a country well-known for its cuisine. People envied that I went to Paris three times in one year, but each time, I was so busy developing and experimenting with cooking that I had no time to look around. Irina Bokova, then the Director-General of UNESCO, attended the UNESCO event I catered. Her attendance meant a lot, and I was grateful she had found the time to participate in the event despite her busy schedule. To thank everyone who came, we prepared the best quality meal we serve at the restaurant. Looking at the expression of contentment on people's faces, I felt as if the world had gotten a bit more plentiful. It was exactly the world I dream of, the world the Buddha spoke of, in which all people share food at the table like family.

The response to temple food was feverous everywhere we went. There was a lot of interest in our unique culture. Just as K-pop isn't only about the music but also the artists' lifestyles, cultures, and philosophies, creating a cultural phenomenon, I believe temple food can also facilitate a philosophical and diplomatic exchange. Food-based communication will play a significant role in sharing Korean culture abroad and uniting the world. But this will require constant study and research of both food and mind. That's how we can make food a vehicle of communication, consideration, contentment, and gratitude.

My Temple Food Bucket List

Temple food is inherent in the practices of Korean temples, converting one's mindset around food into one of gratitude for nature, preventing illness brought on by greed, and brightening the spirit by recovering the self. So, how exactly can we globalize this food practice?

Wouldn't visitors experience more satisfaction staying at the temple, surrounded by nature, and sharing meals with monks? More than simply tasting temple food at a restaurant, staying at a temple and gaining firsthand memories will undoubtedly make people want to return for a second visit. The values and worldview associated with the food will also remain with them for a long time, even after they return to their countries. And this will help spread the food practice to more places worldwide.

The Creation of Taste: From Tradition to Diversity

In human culture, what does it mean to be traditional, and what does it mean to be non-traditional? What does it mean to be conventional and unconventional? To be scientific and unscientific?

The world undergoes rapid change, but humans are still the principal players of life. In the vast history of humankind, traditions have disappeared to be replaced by non-tradition. What is conventional becomes unconventional, and vice versa. New discoveries make unscientific things scientific and vice versa. Life is always in constant change and motion.

If we insist only on tradition, there can be no new tastes. Not only will this make it difficult to evolve food culture, but it may even make it hard to pass on to the next generation. When the natural environment changes, the produce also changes. New cooking methods must follow. But transformation is difficult. Because it's unfamiliar, it's hard to get people to accept it. Behavioral change can only happen when there's also a certain amount of change in the environment. This can make transformation a slow process.

Empathy is being one with the world, and communication is conversing eagerly with the world. When you make food with respect for the world, new flavors and creations emerge.

Traditionally, Korean temple cuisine has no fried dishes like in Japan. But these days, we see new creations like eggplant pasta, potato pizza, vegetarian *jajangmyeon,* and rice burgers. Rather than sticking to tradition, there must be small, flexible changes. Using all five senses and genuinely enjoying temple food can help people love it more. If we add new, unique flavors to a traditional background, that food tradition will survive longer.

Our traditional food can be described as the "food of patience." Steaming, fermenting, and aging all require the art of waiting. *Doenjang* and soy sauce take time to emerge in their natural state. By following this principle, we can make food in a way that's appropriate to the circumstances. If it's too difficult to make this food, one must grow the wisdom of choosing a well-made sauce to purchase. It's no use saying that the best food has a mother's touch. We must develop our palates and learn how to creatively preserve our flavors.

Fermented preserved tofu is one of Korea's traditional foods made by steeping tofu in *doenjang* for three months. This item was priceless when no refrigeration or *banchan* tradition existed, but recent changes have been made. First, perception has changed to the point where we no longer eat it. Many people nowadays try to consume less salt, and this fermented preserved tofu is too salty for the modern taste buds. Second, due to environmental change, tofu often becomes too watery and soft buried in *doenjang*. To address these problems, we now place the tofu in soy sauce and rice syrup for 10 days, drain the water, and then add to the *doenjang* to age for about a week. This new method through continuous trials and study allowed us to maintain our traditional food taste.

A Taste Revolution: Harmonious Creation

Temple food is simple but special. Anyone can eat it without getting indigestion. Its peaceful taste can be shared with anyone. It's easy to overlook its depth because it's so deceptively simple. But if you learn to savor its taste, you can taste its generosity of spirit, too.

People who always dine out complain that their bodies are drenched in condiments. We don't often grow tired of homemade food but quickly get bored of dine-out options, constantly seeking the next new thing. The takeaway food we purchase is often stripped of fresh ingredients and contains at least one artificial ingredient. On top of that, it's way too greasy, contains too much sauce, and has a whole load of processed ingredients to go with it, which is why we quickly get sick of it.

The ingredients for temple food are easy to find as it only uses local, seasonal produce. You need only feel gratitude for the preciousness of life and cook with your heart as you think of yourself and the people you serve.

Last summer, a tall, wide-framed Australian woman visited with her Japanese husband. She tilted her head as she tried the cabbage beet rice, bean sandwich, and mushroom dish. I thought maybe it was because she wasn't used to the style of temple cuisine. At the end of the meal, she suddenly gave a thumbs-up sign while drinking the plum tea.

"Wonderful, oh my god!" she exclaimed, laughing and shaking her head. I laughed along with her and asked why she was reacting this way. She said she had eaten a sizeable steak daily since she was young. This was the first time she had tried temple food. She was surprised by how varied and harmonious vegetarian food could be, marveling at the texture, enjoying the combinations, and anticipating the new flavors. She must have raised her thumb at the lovely pairing of the beet and rice; the sweet symphony of the apple, cucumber, tomato, and lettuce; the fresh abundance of colorful mushrooms and other vegetables; and the happy scent of the single green plum in the tea. I vowed to continue to pour my efforts into sharing this beauty with the world.

The Globalization of Food: Instant Fresh Temple Food

Life is a study. A scientist studies to understand the universe. A teacher studies to teach their pupils. A student studies to comprehend a subject. A business owner studies to sell good products. An employee studies to improve their work life. A parent studies to better fulfill their role as guardian. I study to share temple food.

I spend the most time developing cooking methods to make that possible. That's why we're pouring energy into making fresh instant temple food. As a result of our efforts, we've launched potato pizza, rice burger, and *kimchi japchae*. Recently, there was a workshop for monks cooking temple food. The mutual agreement was that people would be less confused if professional monks could explain the tradition and fusion of temple food. There was a concern that as temple food becomes part of the mainstream, there might be side effects. So, here's the definition that was reached: temple food includes everything made in accordance with temple cooking and follows the Buddha's words on avoiding animal-based ingredients and the Five Pungent Plants. This definition acknowledges that the times change, and so do the ingredients and seasons. This was good news for someone who often gets accused of departing from tradition.

Food culture can't be so strictly defined. No two servings of *doenjang jjigae* are the same because the method of fermenting the beans, the ingredients used, and the person making it are all factors. Food is a mixed cultural art with the chef's heart at the forefront. So how could we insist on making the same food over and over? The globalization of temple food needs creativity and fluidity.

While lecturing at a university, I heard one of the students comment that she buys her children pizza with reluctance and doesn't feel great about it. In the old days, kids' snacks were homemade mung bean pancakes, sweet potatoes, or rice cakes. But today, children want roasted chicken, pizza, and sweet and sour pork. A neighborhood list of restaurants shows a plethora of chicken, Chinese food, and pizza. These foods aren't healthy, but since they're popular worldwide, I thought we could birth a global temple food menu if we put a spin on them. This was how the following revolutionary dishes entered the international food pool.

Rice Burger

The rice burger was one of the dishes that received the most praise after being showcased on the Buddhist TV Network. It's made by putting rice in a rectangular mold to create a patty, then wrapping vegetarian ham, apple, and cabbage dressed in vegetarian tofu sauce in lettuce. The sauce contains a nutty flavor, which makes it both tasty and nutritious. It combines high protein and low calories, making it a fantastic dish for all ages. When we put the dish on the menu of our restaurant, it was as high in demand as the *kimbap*. I long for the day when the rice burger makes a hamburger pale in comparison.

Rice Cake

Everything in the world can be a teacher of life. The rice cake was a dish that one of our students showcased before graduation. It's similar to a deconstructed rice burger. Humans are creative by nature, and my nature keeps inventing new versions of existing cuisine. Stacking rice and vegetables makes the cake a bit heavy, but the dish is reborn as a healthy cake. Instead of sweet, whipped cream, the layers are filled with tofu cream, nuts, and fruits. It looks like a regular cake and tastes just as delicious. What else is an invention but making sugar-free food in a world full of sugar? There's always more sugar than you think, so you must watch with hawk eyes to spot it. How fulfilling it is to see a cake full of fresh ingredients instead of calcium-depriving sugar.

Potato Pizza

There are many ways to make pizza dough, but I chose to use potatoes for their low calories, rich vitamins and minerals, and alkaline properties. First, grind raw potatoes, mix them with local flour, and make a thin dough. Then, spread a layer of steamed mashed potatoes on top. Next, add mushrooms, carrots, cabbage, and raw or steamed pepper, then sprinkle shredded yam like cheese. Bake it to make a nutritious potato pizza. If you want to add cheese, simply use less yam and add cheese.

Vegetarian Ham Kimbap

Kimbap and *tteokbokki* represent Korea's modern cuisine. *Kimbap* is a great field trip snack as it's easy to take anywhere. There are all kinds of varieties to the dish with different fillings. So, how do you reinvent *kimbap* à la temple food? First, ham can be replaced with vegetarian ham made with beans, flour, and salt. It looks and tastes the same as regular ham, so kids have a hard time telling them apart. This makes it an excellent option for children who eat a lot of meat and need to embrace a more vegetarian palate. Next, add burdock, which adds a satisfying texture. Add various vegetables of your choosing. You can also make *banchan* by roasting vegetarian ham, vegetables, and tomatoes. Or add a bunch of vegetables to make a sandwich. Vegetarian ham is tasty and contains a lot of protein, making it a popular item.

Vegetarian *Jajangmyeon* (Black Bean Noodles)

Though black bean sauce noodles originated from China, they were reborn to suit Korean tastes and remain one of the most popular dishes along with ramen. It's so prevalent that people often eat it to celebrate a graduation. If bone broth soup was the common dish of the people during the Joseon period, today, we could say that it's *jajangmyeon*. So, I went to

work to reinvent this popular dish and export it back into the world. Dice potatoes, pumpkin, cabbage, carrots, shiitake, pine mushrooms, and fried tofu. Over high heat, stir-fry the vegetables with black bean paste, starting with the carrots. Once they're cooked, add in some starch mixed with water to thicken the sauce. Boil noodles according to preference. Then, add the finished sauce on top. The scent alone will be enough to make you drool. A dish like this one is the embodiment of fusion food, something that contains passion, harmony, and generosity.

The Future of Temple Food: Temple Food School

Generally speaking, people who love temple food do so for its simple, natural taste, the purity of its philosophy, and the health benefits. It's a mysterious food from the core of Buddhist culture—a food of good deeds that provides happiness and contentment to those who eat it. It's the food of the heart, mind, and body. These factors connect the public with the temple. As a monk who cooks, my mission is to preserve these strengths and reduce the barriers that keep people from connecting with this cuisine.

We live in a world where food is part of our daily culture—even the term "food wars" has been coined. Interest in food is growing rapidly, making up a large part of our mass media. Along with this trend, temple food is also gaining traction as a healthy diet.

Despite this, since temple food comes from the temple, there hasn't been an opportunity to expand the cuisine until now. Though interest is growing, there's a lack of chefs and other experts. The infrastructure to support further development and growth isn't there either. There's insufficient marketing for the existing programs, and government funding is minimal. We also need systemization, modernization, and business savvy for the globalization of temple food. The temple food of the past was incredibly natural, yet for the food to be shared, we need to keep up with the times. Modernization doesn't mean getting rid of tradition. Korean food didn't disappear because we stopped cooking rice over a fire.

What we need most are chefs. They must learn the philosophy behind the food, study the nature of each ingredient and how to gather mountain herbs, research harvesting and cooking methods, and develop new technology and infrastructure. These things must be taught at a professional culinary school. Only through this process can temple food take its place as a cultural product representing Korea.

Temple food has only just taken its first step towards these goals. Many of our chefs end up working at traditional Korean restaurants operated by big companies after gaining basic experience. But expertise in the tradition of temple food cannot just be a line on a resume. In a society where competition is everything, temple food is no exception. We practitioners of the temple food movement often feel inferior to wealthy corporations paying thousands more, although our positions are also salaried and have the same working conditions. This is why we need a school for temple food. Those attending the school will gain knowledge, wisdom, and practical experience, making them capable chefs upon graduation. Every foreign chef who visits Guemsuam Temple comments that it's wonderful that chefs can get their own ingredients by going out into the fields and mountains.

Growing their own produce at the school will also make aspiring chefs appreciate the value of sweat. They will learn all their characteristics and medicinal qualities as they watch the plants grow. By learning to respect all life, they will be able to cook with a pure heart wherever they go. They won't play games with food and will only use natural additives. Since they will have already learned about the inappropriate nature of artificial condiments and the superiority of natural ones, they won't choose to make junk food. Anyone running a temple food operation will be able to work with quality chefs. Personally, all this makes establishing a school of temple food feel like an important responsibility.

This mission is essential because, through temple food, we can share our warm hearts with one another, help our neighbors grow healthier and happier, and make the earth suffer less. In order to plant the roots of this food, we need to spread its seeds. So once again, I sit down in front of my computer to make healthy recipes oozing with the sauce of benevolence.

Rice Burger

Even the culture and tradition of Korean temple cuisine is evolving to introduce more creative menu items. Brown rice is a healthy alternative to other carbohydrates. This rice burger, inspired by hamburgers, is a great lunch option, especially for kids. Because you can use leftover cold rice, it's easy to make rice "buns."

Ingredients

4 cups cooked brown rice, cooled

2 tomatoes

3 ounces green cabbage

1.5 ounces lotus root

5 shiitake mushrooms

1 ounce carrot

2 large potatoes

1 tofu block

½ cup soaked black soybeans, boiled for 20 minutes and drained

Salt, sesame oil, *gukganjang* (soup soy sauce) for seasoning

Cooking oil

Directions

1. Season the rice with salt and sesame oil. Press it into a square mold or shape it with your hands to make rice buns. Pan-fry them in oil until golden brown on both sides.
2. Thinly slice the tomatoes and julienne the cabbage.

3. Peel and thinly slice the lotus root, and then grill in a dry pan without oil.

4. Chop the mushrooms, season with soup soy sauce and sesame oil, then pan-fry.

5. Chop the carrot and pan-fry with a pinch of salt.

6. Grate the potatoes and squeeze out the water. Wrap the tofu in a cheesecloth and squeeze out the water while crumbling it. Mix the potato and tofu together. Season with salt and sesame oil. Press the mixture into the mold to shape into patties or shape it with your hands. Pan-fry them in oil until golden brown on each side.

7. Pound the soybeans in a mortar, season with salt, and shape into thin patties. The soybeans are a great vegan substitute for meat.

8. To assemble a nutritious rice burger, start with one rice "bun," layer with a black bean patty, tomato, cabbage, lotus root slice, mushroom, carrot, potato, and tofu patty, and then top with another rice "bun."

Brown Rice *Kimbap*

(Hyeonmi Kimbap)

It is fun to watch how *kimbap* evolves. *Kimbap* is a convenient food everyone enjoys. *Kimbap* brings back memories of the excitement the night before school field trips in my childhood. This *kimbap* recipe makes it even more enjoyable and nutritious by using brown rice and healthy vegetables. *Kimbap* is one of my favorite foods, so I often picnic with *kimbap* made with brown rice and wild greens. It was the first menu item to run out when we had a Lunch Box event at Balwoo Gongyang temple food restaurant.

Ingredients

3 cups uncooked brown rice

4 large sheets *yubu* (fried tofu skin)

2 medium *ueong* (burdock) roots

2 carrots

1 bunch spinach or other greens

1 uncut *danmuji* (pickled radish for *kimbap*) or 10 pre-cut pieces

10 long strips vegetarian sausage/ham

10 sheets *gim* (dried seaweed sheets)

Salt, sesame oil, *gukganjang* (soup soy sauce), *jocheong* (rice syrup), sesame seeds for seasoning

Sauce for burdock roots:

3 tablespoons soaked black soybeans

2 cups water

10 small pieces dried kelp

10 dried shiitake mushrooms

3 tablespoons *gukganjang* (soup soy sauce)

Directions

1. The key to good *kimbap* is well-cooked rice. Cook the rice using slightly less water than usual to make the rice fluffy. When it's still hot, season with salt and sesame oil.

2. Blanch the fried tofu skins in boiling water to remove surface oil, squeeze out the water, and slice them into approximately ½-inch-wide strips. Season with salt and sesame oil, and lightly pan-fry so the seasoning can penetrate through.

3. Make the sauce for the burdock roots. Boil the black beans in 2 cups of water for about 20 minutes, then remove the beans and keep the liquid. Add the kelp and mushrooms to the bean broth and cook for another 7 minutes. Remove the mushrooms and kelp, reserving the mushrooms. Add the soup soy sauce to the liquid and boil for another minute.

4. Peel the outer skin of the burdock roots by scraping it off with a knife, and cut the roots into ¼-inch-thick, long strips that are similar in length to the seaweed sheets. Braise the burdock roots in the prepared sauce and rice syrup to taste.

5. Squeeze the liquid out of the reserved mushrooms and cut them into thin strips. Season with soup soy sauce and sesame oil, and lightly pan-fry.

6. Slice the carrots into ¼-inch-thick, long strips and stir-fry in sesame oil, seasoning with salt.

7. Blanch the spinach in salted boiling water, then squeeze out the water. Season with soup soy sauce, sesame oil, and sesame seeds.

8. Cut the pickled radish into thin strips, similar to the carrots.

9. Cut the vegetarian sausage/ham into thin strips, and pan-fry.

10. To assemble, evenly spread seasoned rice on the seaweed, leaving about 1 ½ inches of space at the top. Place all the prepared ingredients in the middle section, and roll tightly all the way, tucking in the fillings. It's important not to use too much rice. It's better to use less rice and more vegetable fillings.

Sweet & Sour Mushrooms

(Neungi Beoseot Gangjeong)

I love the fragrance of *neungi beoseot* (shingled hedgehog mushrooms) so much that I keep them inside my room in lieu of incense. The fragrant mushrooms converted into crispy sweet morsels are enough to attract the taste buds of pickiest eaters.

Ingredient:

4 to 5 dried *neungi beoseot* (shingled hedgehog mushrooms) or dried shiitake, white, or king oyster mushrooms
Gukganjang (soup soy sauce) and sesame oil for seasoning
Potato starch
Oil for frying
½ ounce pumpkin seeds, coarsely chopped
½ ounce sunflower seeds, coarsely chopped

Batter:
1 cup flour
½ cup potato starch, plus more for dredging
Pinch salt
⅔ cup water

Sauce:
1 tablespoon *gochujang*
2 tablespoons regular soy sauce

1 tablespoon *jocheong* (rice syrup)

1 tablespoon *maesilcheong* (green plum syrup)

Directions

1. Shingled hedgehog mushrooms are high in fiber and water content, so they give you a feeling of fullness and help you with weight control and digestion. To prepare the dried mushrooms, brush the mushrooms to remove any dirt, and soak in cold water until soft. Squeeze out excess water, reserving the soaking water for later use in soups or stews.

2. Cut the mushrooms into bite-sized pieces. Further remove moisture from the mushroom pieces with a clean, dry cloth or paper towel to prevent the hot oil from splashing when frying.

3. Lightly season the mushroom pieces with soup soy sauce and sesame oil.

4. Prepare the batter. Sift together the flour, potato starch, and salt. Add the water and mix well.

5. Dredge the mushrooms in potato starch. Dip them in the batter and fry them twice in the oil until crispy.

6. Mix and simmer the sauce ingredients together over medium-low heat. Lightly toss the fried mushrooms in the sauce. To maintain their crispiness, do not soak them in the sauce.

7. Put the mushrooms on a plate and garnish with the pumpkin and sunflower seeds.

Note: In the springtime, try fragrant wild greens such as *naengi* (shepherd's purse) instead of mushrooms for a fragrant and crispy treat.

Closing Words

It is said that one sees as much as one has experienced. I joined Guemsuam Temple as a young monk, practicing away from the world. Now, I'm communicating with the world as I look at myself, the world, and the universe.

By a fortuitous turn of events, I was invited to a temple food exhibition in Seattle. It was there that I first opened my eyes to the possibilities of this cuisine. This experience led me to UNESCO's Korea Day event, further opening my eyes to the wisdom of sharing temple food with the world while delivering a message of respect for all life.

It could be said all things in life are interconnected. Some connections and patterns of life are organic and inseparable, while others change over time. When there's suffering and dissatisfaction in our current lives, we try changing and improving our diet or behaviors. All these actions we take in the interest of self-reflection and self-improvement are a practice and a meditation.

Sunlight doesn't seduce us, but artificial light leads us to disability and suffering. Though we may try to stop eating meat, cut out alcohol, give up smoking, and become a vegetarian, it's no small feat to get rid of the shadow of habits we've been carrying all our lives. We fall for flashy and fancy things, sinking into a delightful, sugary fantasy. The shadow of desire always accompanies the darkness that covers up true wisdom.

We wish to be healthy all our lives, and we can't ever give up on that. We can give up happiness, but we can't give up health. Throughout history, this has been humanity's greatest, most desperate desire. So, when we become sick, we start paying attention to our diet and begin meditating to balance the mind. Both temple food and vegetarian food have received attention for the same reason. But without proper care and sincerity, it's hard to gain health of mind and body. We need to clean out our minds and bodies by giving them the nutrition of love.

Our body, just like all things in universe, is made up of the four elements of earth, water, fire, and wind, and operates according to *Oheng* of wood, fire, earth, metal, and water energies. If we've lived under the shadow of the five aggregates, we'll have to wash away their contaminants to escape their restraints. We must be renewed with gratitude each day, serve from that space, and continue to connect. Practicing this every day in the same way we eat food every day brightens the mind and body.

For some time now, I have been called "*Seunim* that cooks (요리하는 스님)," a cooking monk. Some people thought it a pity that a monk would only occupy herself with food. But the path of practice is diverse. The one I walk is that of meditation through food. It would be hypocritical to say that a good life is one of eating, sleeping, and releasing well while practicing a poor diet. So, I'm happily practicing and communicating with temple food. This is how I can repay the world's kindness and grow closer to the Buddha's generosity.

When we are clean within, we'll treat our food kindlier, and our thoughts will spread out into the world not as words but as light. By embracing joy as our food and living a life of light, we will all begin to follow the wisdom of the Buddha.

I dedicate these words to all those who took the time to read them despite their simplicity—to all those who keep practicing and to all the monks carrying on their beautiful discipline. And lastly, I dedicate this book to all those who have yet to discover their precious value.

Putting my hands together,
Venerable Dae-Ahn
Mount Jirisan, May 2012

Venerable Dae-Ahn

Temple Cuisine Master, Jogye Order of Korean Buddhism

Doctor of Science, Food & Nutrition, Dogguk University

guemsuam.or.kr/eng

ALSO AVAILABLE FROM ALPHA SISTERS PUBLISHING

Don't Be a B*tch, Be an Alpha: How to Unlock Your Magic, Play Big, and Change the World

Return: Korea's Rituals of Death, Spirits, and Ancestors

Budoji: A Tale of the Divine City of Ancient Korea with an Overview of Korean Shamanism

I Have Come on a Lonely Path: Memoir of a Shaman

Korean Folktales: Four Feminist Retellings

The End

Printed in Great Britain
by Amazon

48119455R00126